Death at the Wedding

Madelaine Duke

Retold by L A Hill

Illustrated by Paul Wright

NELSON

THOMAS NELSON AND SONS LTD
Nelson House Mayfield Road
Walton-on-Thames Surrey KT12 5PL

51 York Place
Edinburgh EH1 3JD

Yi Xiu Factory Building
Unit 05-06 5th Floor
65 Sims Avenue Singapore 1438

Thomas Nelson (Hong Kong) Ltd
Watson Estate Block A 13 Floor
Watson Road Causeway Bay Hong Kong

THOMAS NELSON (NIGERIA) LTD
8 Ilupeju Bypass PMB 21303 Ikeja Lagos

© *L A Hill 1978*
First published 1978
Reprinted 1979, 1982

ISBN 0 17 555265 7
NCN 740-8648-2

Filmset by Filmtype Services Limited. Scarborough.

Printed in Hong Kong

1. What is the name of the person who tells the story? What is his/her profession, and where does he/she work?

2. There are three main events in the story: the death of Great-aunt Theresa, Fraser's illness and Elsa's problem. What is the main connection between all three, and how is it that the person who tells the story gets mixed up with all three problems?

3. Certain things happen to make the person who tells the story suspicious. Describe three of these.

4. What in the story tells you that the person who is telling it is sympathetic toward immigrants from Asia or the Caribbean in Britain?

5. How did the bad person in the story expect to get money as a result of his/her evil deeds? Why was this money needed by the bad person?

One

The wedding ceremony was nearly finished. The old church smelled of fresh leaves and flowers.

I found my mind wandering. I was thinking about some of my patients, and then remembering my childhood with the bride. Joanna and I had been close friends since our school days; I hoped we would still continue like that. Of course there'd be some changes. Jeremy and his job would change Joanna's pattern of living; or would it? I wondered whether Joanna would stop being an actress now.

Then I remembered something else. When I had arrived at the church, Joan, the bride's mother, had been smoking a cigarette. She had been drawing the smoke deep into her lungs when her son had come rushing out of the church.

"Mother, do go in and sit down." Fraser had held out his hand. "And let me put out this cigarette. You'll be coughing right through the wedding ceremony."

Joan Camp had filled her lungs with smoke again before giving up the cigarette. "Don't worry, Fraser."

"Look, it worries me. I thought you'd given up smoking. But you're chain-smoking forty a day, or more. It's time your husband did something about it."

"Fraser, please leave Leon out of it."

"I don't understand it. If I were a famous doctor like Leon I'd be worried about my wife's smoker's cough."

"Well, you're not Leon."

Perhaps that scene didn't mean much. It was not surprising that Joan should feel the strain of organising her daughter's wedding and smoke more as a result. However, I hoped that Fraser would speak to his stepfather about his mother's smoking. It would be wise to X-ray her chest.

After the ceremony I looked for my sister, Liz.

"She's gone to fetch the car," someone said.

"I thought we were going to walk to the reception."

"No, we can't. We have to take the old lady . . . you know, Great-aunt Theresa from Australia. Fraser was going to drive her there, but he's had to go home."

"Why? What's the matter?"

"He's ill. Dr Camp said it's jaundice and that we mustn't tell anyone. He doesn't want Joanna to know."

It was just possible that Joanna wouldn't notice her brother's absence until the end of the reception. Though the three rooms at the Crown Hotel were connected, the three hundred guests split into almost separate parties. Those in the first room wouldn't see the people in the second and third rooms. The guests in the second and third rooms wouldn't see the ceremony of cutting the cake, but they'd be able to hear the speeches through the loudspeakers.

We took Great-aunt Theresa to the Crown Hotel and put her in a chair.

The old lady, watching Joanna and Jeremy receive the last of their guests, was enjoying herself. "That's how a bride should look. Nice and clean." The strong Australian voice went well with Miss Theresa's bright red hat. "I know Joanna's got to put a lot of stuff on her face when she's working, but there's no need for it when she isn't on the stage. Soap and water's the best thing. Of course, as I told Joanna, I have nothing against eye make-up; that does something for a woman, even at my age . . . I'll be eighty next month. Now, don't waste your time on me, Joanna. Go and look after your guests. I'll get myself some food."

"Fraser's supposed to be looking after you. Where's he gone?" Joanna said.

"I don't need looking after." Miss Theresa took Joanna's hand. "I'd much rather help myself."

"But Fraser. . . ."

"Do your job, dear, and let Fraser do his. He's very good ."

at this sort of thing." Miss Theresa got up and went to the long tables where the food was.

Fraser was chairman of the Petrie Corporation, the big family company in Australia which his grandfather had built up from nothing. He had had to become chairman when he was very young, because his father had drowned when he was thirty. He'd been the only son. His father had had no family except his sister Theresa.

Joanna, Fraser's sister, had wanted to become an actress and live in England with her mother and stepfather.

After the reception had been going on for about an hour, a waiter came up to me.

"Dr North?" he said.

"Yes," I answered.

"There's a telephone call for you, Doctor."

I got up.

"That's funny," I thought.

I hadn't given any number where I could be found. Dr Markham was on duty; but I followed the waiter past the crowded tables, across the room, to the door.

The waiter led me up some back stairs. "Dr Camp asked me to get you."

"Then I'm not wanted on the telephone?"

"No, Miss . . . . It's the old lady. A relation of the bride's, I believe. . . . She's had a heart attack."

They were standing around anxiously like actors before the play starts. Mr Smythe, the manager of the Crown; Joan Camp, greedily smoking one of her long cigarettes; Dr Leon Camp at the window, his thick grey hair dark against the sunlight.

There was a medical bag on the armchair, a box of coramine ampoules, one of them broken open, and a hypodermic syringe on the table. I saw the small body of Miss Theresa Petrie on the bed.

"Norah," said Dr Camp, turning towards me, "forgive

me for troubling you in this way, but we need your help. We mustn't spoil Joanna's wedding. She's been fond of her great-aunt, and it's almost time for the speeches. . . ."

Dr Camp went to stand beside me at the bed. "She had angina," he said. "I'd been looking after her for five years or more. I was afraid the wedding might be too much for her." He looked at the hypodermic syringe. "I took my bag with me, but I'm afraid that this time the coramine didn't save her."

"I'm sorry," I said. "What would you like me to do?"

"Take care of everything for us. Mr Smythe feels that a death at his hotel is likely to upset the people who are staying here."

"Sir." The Manager looked worried. "I'm prepared to wait."

"It's all right," said Dr Camp quickly. "It's been decided. Mr Smythe has telephoned Gilberts, the local undertakers. They should be here soon."

"Leon, please." Joan Camp wiped the tears from her eyes. "Must we do it? Poor Theresa. To have her collected like a. . . ."

"Joan, you know we can't do anything else."

She shook her head. "It seems so unkind."

"My dear, we've got to think of Joanna. The undertakers will take good care of Theresa."

"But Joanna will notice."

"We'll tell her that her great-aunt got a bit tired and went to the cottage for a rest." Camp picked up the box of cigarettes which was lying beside his medical bag and offered it to his wife.

Joan took a cigarette without thinking. Mr Smythe lit a match for her.

Camp looked at his watch. "It's getting late." He opened his bag, searched in some papers, and took some forms out. "Norah, will you deal with Gilberts' men?"

"Yes, of course."

"That's kind of you." He put the forms on the table and began to fill in the one on top. "I'm sorry to ruin the party for you. But I couldn't think of anyone who'd deal with everything more sensibly. Besides, none of my doctor friends downstairs knew Theresa." He signed the death certificate and handed it to me. "That's for the undertakers. Tell them I'll telephone them when the guests have gone."

Dr Camp took his wife by the arm. "Come on, my dear." At the door he turned. "I'm afraid I'll have to trouble you with more forms, Norah. Theresa wished to be cremated."

"Cremated?" Joan said in surprise. "She didn't talk to me about. . . ."

"She discussed it with me when she was ill last autumn. Norah, perhaps I'd better tell the others that you've gone to see how Fraser is."

When I was alone in the bedroom, I began to think. If I had been in Dr Camp's place, I wouldn't have been able to act so quickly and efficiently. But of course he was twice my age, and much more experienced. He had been very thoughtful, and determined not to spoil Joanna's wedding.

It was quite natural that he should have called me in. He'd known me from childhood. And when I'd been a medical student, he had taken an interest in my progress and discussed unusual cases with me. What he asked of me now was perfectly reasonable. All the same, I had not expected to have to deal with the problems of cremation.

I had expected that Miss Theresa would be buried. If that had been the arrangement, the death certificate, signed by Dr Camp, and registration of the death would have been all that was needed. But the rules for cremation were more complicated and strict.

There would have to be a cremation certificate signed by two doctors, the one who'd been attending the deceased and another — myself. The law said that the second doctor had to question everyone who'd been present at the death, including the attending doctor; and carry out a full examination of the outside of the body. However, in Miss Theresa's case there would be no problems.

I guessed that the undertakers wouldn't produce the necessary forms before next morning. It meant that I'd have to stay at Southdown Village that night. I'd better telephone the surgery; one of the partners would have to take my place that evening.

There was one thing I could do while waiting for the undertakers' men. I went to the bed and touched Miss Theresa's face. It felt cool but not cold. I opened the collar of the old lady's red blouse and looked at the neck of the body; in this case a full examination would have been rather silly.

I picked up the death certificate. Dr Camp had given the cause of death as "heart failure". I had no reason to doubt this. A woman of almost eighty, with angina. It's what I would have expected. And the things on the table told their own story; the box of coramine, with one ampoule missing; beside it, the broken ampoule and hypodermic syringe. Here was proof of Dr Camp's thoughtfulness. Since he couldn't have taken away from the old lady the pleasure of attending the wedding, he'd prepared for the worst. He'd taken his bag with him. He'd watched her, and he'd managed to get her out of the crowd before people noticed her condition and became worried.

There were sounds of cheering from below. The cutting of the cake. Judging by the applause and the laughter, Joanna and Jeremy were having a good time. With luck, they'd continue to do so.

Suddenly the door opened. It was my sister Liz.

"So that's it," she said, closing the door behind her.

"Go away." I didn't know how to deal with my sister. "We're trying to keep this quiet. Miss Theresa. . . ."

"She was so nice." Liz had gone to the bed and was studying the small body. "It's a pity. I wish she hadn't known."

"Known what?"

"Well — it wouldn't have been so hard on her if she'd died in her sleep, would it?"

"Oh, stop it. She must have died quickly."

"How quickly?"

"I — I don't know. Within minutes, I suppose."

"Minutes can last a long time."

Not for the first time, I felt disturbed by my young sister's sudden flashes of insight. "Look here, a very old lady has died. It's normal. It's part of living. So don't let your imagination run away with you."

"I'm not imagining things," said Liz. "She knew she was dying. You can see that from the look on her face. And she was frightened — really frightened."

Two

It was the next morning, and I was back in London, seeing my patients at my surgery.

One of them was Mr Jeff. He was wearing an expensive leather coat over a dirty shirt.

"You're not really ill, you know," I said to him.

"Oh, come on, Doctor. I haven't got any red blood. That's why I feel tired."

"You feel tired because you're too fat. Try eating less and. . . ."

Jeff smiled. "Look, Doctor, all I want is my certificate to say that I'm too ill to work, and some medicine to make me stronger."

"I'm not going to give you a certificate. You're quite fit for work, and you don't need any medicine either."

"I saw a programme on television about medicines which make you stronger."

"If you think you're not getting proper treatment, change your doctor."

"You don't mean that, Doctor, do you? I'm not saying that you're not giving me the right treatment, am I? It's just that I lose money if I take a job, you see. I get more when I'm unemployed. From the government, you see."

"I see all right. Is there any reason why I should pay for you to live without working, Mr Jeff?"

"You mean out of your taxes, Doctor?"

"Yes, that's exactly what I mean."

"Have you had a bad day, then?" asked Jeff sympathetically. "It's very sad that a beautiful girl like you has to work so hard."

"Go away. And ask my nurse to bring me the files which are on her desk."

Jeff got up. "All right, Doctor. . . . The black girl out there? Do you call her a nurse? . . . All right, all right. I wasn't trying to be rude. . . . Do you like my coat? A friend of mine gets them cheaply. It's his business. Would you like me to get one for you? Twenty pounds — less than it costs to make them. What do you say?"

"Out!"

"Whatever you say, Doctor," Mr Jeff said, and got out surprisingly quickly in spite of all his fat.

I laughed aloud. Well, Jeff wasn't my worst patient. His parents had been very poor, so he hadn't had the best start in life. He'd become my patient about three years before. He'd fallen off a tree and hurt his back. He'd fallen while rescuing an old woman's cat. He was always willing to help people who needed help, and always in trouble with the police for stealing things. His friend with the leather coat business didn't sound very honest, either.

Elsa, my West Indian nurse, brought the files in, and I called the next patient.

When I finished seeing my patients that day, it was after nine o'clock in the evening.

I took off my white coat and picked up my bag. I turned off the lights and went out through the waiting room. The street door was closed and Elsa's key was in the lock. That was strange; Elsa should have left two hours before.

I found her in the little kitchen at the back of the hall, cleaning the gas stove. Her dark head was bent forward and the white hat had slipped, showing the dark skin of the neck. For a moment I wondered whether I was imagining things. But I was not: on the left side of that smooth neck was an ugly wound which looked as if it had been there for several days.

"It's nothing. Really," Elsa said. "It was my collar . . . it rubbed my neck."

"Before you go home, I'd like to look at it," I said. "Do you mind?"

For a moment Elsa looked almost frightened. Then she nodded. "All right. But it's nothing. Really."

Elsa followed me, sat down and took off her hat. The wound couldn't have been caused by the rubbing of a collar. I could see some nasty cuts, which looked as if they'd been made with a sharp instrument.

"It won't hurt, Elsa. I'll put a bandage on it. And I'd like to give you an injection of penicillin. All right?"

"Yes."

While I worked on her, the girl sat still. She wasn't nervous. But she was very depressed, and that was most unusual for her.

"Who did this thing to you?" I said.

Elsa shook her head.

"Someone attacked you. Anyone can see that. Someone really nasty. He nearly killed you. I wish you'd tell me about it."

"I can't." Suddenly tears were running down Elsa's face. "I can't."

"Singh might need help."

"Singh?" Elsa's head went up suddenly. "You don't believe that Singh did it? He'd never hurt anyone. He's wonderful. . . . And now . . . it's all finished."

"Your engagement?"

"He doesn't want me any more. He's gone."

"Where?"

"I don't know. He's left the hospital."

"He'll have taken another job in a hospital. Perhaps we can. . . ."

"It's no good. It's no good, Doctor. He won't see me. It's my fault."

I couldn't believe that. Elsa wasn't the kind of girl who'd get into a situation where she was nearly murdered of her own free will. She'd been so happy planning her marriage with the young Asian doctor from Uganda. She'd been excited about finding a cheap flat, about furnishing and decorating it. Elsa was sensible, intelligent and efficient. Whatever had gone wrong wouldn't be her fault.

"It's late." I felt sure that Elsa would say no more about the attack. Not now. "Come home with me. Stay with me for a few days."

"Thanks." She turned away. "I can't. I've got to be at my place." She sounded calm but hopeless. "I've got to be there."

"Don't you understand? The person who attacked you is dangerous."

"Leave me alone! Don't interfere. I — I'm sorry, Doctor. I didn't mean. . . . Don't worry. Please. He's not like you think. He knows what he's doing. . . . He knows."

I knew the police inspector at Paddington Police Station, and after thinking about Elsa for a long time, I went to see him the next evening.

The policeman at the desk was a patient of mine. He asked no questions when I asked for Inspector Barrington. He said the Inspector was still in his office. He'd telephone to tell him that I was on my way up.

Barrington met me at the door. He offered me one of the two chairs at a small table in a corner of the office and took the other.

"You're looking very charming, Dr North," he said.

"Thank you. I'm going out to dinner."

"Have you come about one of your patients?"

"No. I'm worried about Elsa, the West Indian girl who works for us. She does just about everything, from cleaning to keeping the files. She's normally a very happy girl."

I told Barrington about the wound on Elsa's neck, about the broken engagement and the girl's refusal to say anything about the person who had attacked her.

Barrington listened carefully and then said, "You're not asking me to give her police protection?"

"Elsa's not a government minister, unfortunately for her. She's not an important person. I just want to know what *can* be done."

"Officially, nothing. The girl's made no complaint. She hasn't accused anyone. Quite the opposite; she's told even you to keep out of it."

"I believe she's in danger."

"I expect you're right, Dr North. Unfortunately, she's not the only one. We get a lot of calls from girls who say their men have threatened to kill them. Believe me, when I send a man to that kind of house the girl and the man just complain of police interference. It's happened again and again. And I'm speaking of cases where there's actually been a complaint. Elsa wouldn't accept help even from you."

"She's very frightened."

"I wish I could help more. But at the moment there's little I can do. Until. . . ."

"Until the madman kills her?" I immediately regretted my sharpness.

"I understand how you feel," said Barrington, kindly.

"I'll ask our men to have a look at the girl's house whenever they can."

"Thank you." I got up. I couldn't expect more. Barrington had too few men for the job, but was doing it very successfully. The Inspector wouldn't forget Elsa.

He opened the door for me. "A couple of months ago there was an attack on another West Indian, a nice, quiet girl. We haven't yet succeeded in finding the man; the girl refused to help us. If you get a chance, tell Elsa about the other girl. She almost died."

I had been invited to dinner at the Camps' house that evening. I'd always been fond of it. It was part of my childhood, holding memories of many pleasures.

There were beautiful pieces of furniture in it which Joan had brought back from Australia when she'd married Dr Camp. But some of her pieces had disappeared. They'd been replaced by furniture which Dr Camp had bought. He had a taste for highly decorated eighteenth-century French furniture, which didn't fit in at all well with the simple English pieces; yet it was this curious mixture which gave the Camps' house its special charm.

Because of Miss Theresa's death the dinner for Joanna and Jeremy was almost a family occasion. I was the only person from outside. Dr Camp said that Fraser could have come; he was feeling better. But he'd persuaded him to stay in Sussex and rest until he'd got over the worst stage of his jaundice. Joan and Leon Camp themselves served the dinner. Tubby, their Australian servant, was at the cottage, taking care of Fraser.

"Poor fellow," said Dr Camp. "He won't have anything to do. I doubt that he's opened a book since he left school. He and Joanna never had any tastes that they shared. And that doesn't appear to have changed either."

"It doesn't matter to us, Daddy," said Joanna. "We understand one another."

"Yes, you communicate. So do cats and mice."

"Be fair." Joanna laughed. "Our relations are more comfortable. They're based on companionable silence."

"Can she *ever* be silenced?" asked Dr Camp.

Jeremy took Joanna's hand. "I'd hate her to be silent. I like the sound of her voice, on the stage and off."

"If we stay here much longer," said Joanna, "I'll have no voice left. The room's thick with smoke. Mum, you've had six cigarettes with your food. It's very silly."

"You're right. I won't have any more."

"You'll stop?"

"Well . . . until after breakfast."

"That's something." Joanna rose from the table. "Let's have coffee in the living room. I'll make it."

I stayed behind to help. Joanna and I were alone for the first time since the day before her wedding.

"Mum's begun to look old, Norah," she said.

"She's fifty."

"That's not old nowadays. She's lost a lot of weight, hasn't she?"

"Yes, she's thinner. The trouble is that some people who smoke a lot don't eat enough."

"She used to smoke less than twenty a day."

"It's a lot more now. Norah, there must be a reason for it. What is the cause?"

"You should discuss it with your father. He's a doctor and he knows her best."

"Of course. You're right. I know he works long hours, but he'll have to have more time for Mum. He'll have to deal with her."

"He may not be able to."

"A lot of his patients have given up smoking. He even stopped Mum once."

"I doubt that it was your father who stopped her. She couldn't smoke because she was too ill at that time."

"Well, something's got to be done about her. Perhaps Fraser will help; he's very good with her."

"How long is he staying in England?"

"Until the autumn . . . if nothing serious happens in Australia. Daddy's driving down to Sussex at the week-end. I'm sure Fraser will come back to London with him. He doesn't like the country."

After dinner Dr Camp spoke about the state of Britain. "I am glad I am too old to witness the final destruction of this country," he said. "England isn't a country of Englishmen any more. If you look at the faces in the streets — well, we're no better than a colony of Asia or Africa. The quality of the things we have to live with has gone down terribly: food, furniture, cars, buildings. Things are no longer cheap and nasty; almost everything's become *expensive* and nasty. As to our hospitals — their staffs, their laboratories — they're even worse."

Three

The next day I went to see one of my patients in Paddington. On the way I remembered what Dr Camp had said about Asians and Africans. It was true that there were a lot of black and brown people in Edgware Road. They made the place look brighter and more interesting. It was a pity that people of Dr Camp's age could not get used to the changes.

My patient in Paddington was a young man who had been a good footballer, but now he was paralysed, so that he could not walk without help.

When I rang the bell, Mr Jeff came to the door to let me in. Billy had been alone in the house, so Mr Jeff had come to sit with him. Billy was lying on a bed by the window. He looked happy.

"Cup of tea, Doctor?" he asked.

"Yes, thanks." I sat down on the bed beside him. I could see all the way down the street. The people who lived in the houses there called them George Cottages. The owners had divided the big old houses into three flats and spent money on better windows.

Mr Jeff went and brought the tea.

"You've got a wonderful view from here," I said.

"Yes," said Mr Jeff. "Saturday's the best day. You know Paddy, who sells flowers in the street? On Saturdays, he and his friends put boxes in the street and have gambling games on them. They get crowds of people to play, and Billy can watch from here with his binoculars. If the police come, Paddy and his friends hide the cards. It's very easy, because the cards are quite small."

We talked for a few more minutes, and then Billy mentioned Elsa.

"Elsa Barbuda?" I asked.

"That's right," said Mr Jeff. "The West Indian girl who works at your surgery."

"She's a friend of yours, Billy?"

"Well, I met her at your surgery, and since she's moved to George Cottages she's been coming in to see me on her way home."

Of course. A well-known footballer who would never play again. Elsa would feel sorry for him. She was good with such patients. She was sensitive to anyone who had disadvantages, because there must have been times when she had suffered from the disadvantages of being coloured.

"Why do you call me Mr Jeff, Doctor?" Jeff asked suddenly. "Why don't you just call me J.J.? Everyone else does."

"All right, J.J.," I said. "I'll do that."

"Well, I must go," said J.J. "I've got some work to do."

When he had gone I said, "Billy, there's something useful you could do for me."

"What's that?" he asked eagerly.

"From here you can see the house where Elsa lives?"

"Yes. It's the one with the window boxes."

"I'd like you to keep watch on it."

"Like a detective?"

"Yes. Could you?"

"With these binoculars I can see everything that's happening. What is it you want me to find out, then?"

"You'd have to keep it secret."

"Of course."

"About a week ago Elsa was attacked and hurt."

"She had a bandage on her neck," said Billy. "I asked her about it. She said it was nothing."

"That wasn't true. Someone hurt her. On purpose. But she's so frightened that she won't talk."

"There are some people around here who attack women and steal their money," said Billy. "But they usually choose old women. And fights . . . well, they're between men."

"It was nothing like that," I told him. "I think Elsa's got mixed up with a man who's dangerous. I think she's still seeing him."

"It sounds nasty."

"It is. That's why I want to know about him."

"I'll watch out, Doctor. I've got plenty of time, haven't I?"

"How good are the street lights in George Cottages?"

"I see what you mean. If he goes to Elsa's after dark, I wouldn't be able to see his face. Not properly. But I'd get an idea of what he's like. Perhaps if I asked Elsa. . . ."

"No, Billy. You mustn't."

"That's right." He began to see the difficulties. "If I see somebody who doesn't live near here, how do I find out about him?"

"All I want just now is a description of anyone like that."

"There's not much you can do with it, is there?"

"The police might be interested."

"Yes," he said doubtfully. "But J.J. and the boys are the ones who could really help."

I wondered whether I'd been wise to tell Billy. I didn't like the idea of getting the help of "the boys", the street traders who were gambling and making a living out of crime.

"You know, Doctor, they're all right." Billy had guessed my thoughts. "I'll do all I can, but if we have any trouble, you only have to tell me and the boys will help us. If there's one thing they hate it's the kind of person who hurts nice girls like Elsa."

Four

While the Camps were at their Sussex cottage with Fraser, Joanna and I were spending the Sunday afternoon at their house off Baker Street. We were doing the jobs for which there had been no time before the wedding — dividing lots of clothes and books into piles to be thrown away and parcels to be moved to Joanna's new flat in Hurlingham Gardens.

It took a long time, because Joanna had to try all her clothes on to see whether she wanted to keep them, and we argued when she wanted to give me expensive coats or furs. As we were about to leave, Joanna suddenly said, "Oh, the furniture. We've got to go up to the attic. I promised Mum that I'd tell her which pieces I wanted."

"Can't you do it another time?"

"No, let's finish it all now. It won't take long."

I knew it would take a long time as soon as we got into the

attic and I saw what was there. While Joanna chose pieces of furniture, I wandered about the attic. Suddenly I saw a beautiful table which had once stood beside the fireplace in the sitting room. It was years since I'd last seen it, but I was certain of one thing: it had not been damaged then. Now the top was permanently spoiled by two long, deep cigarette burns.

"Look at this," I called to Joanna.

"So that's where it got to." When she saw the burns she too was shocked. "What a terrible waste!"

"Who'd do such a thing?"

"None of us. We don't smoke. And it can't have been Mum."

"She's the smoker."

"Exactly. There's something I learned when I was an actress. A lot of actors smoke, especially when they're in strange theatres, playing to audiences they don't know. And it was always the occasional smokers who burnt holes in their clothes or the furniture; because they'd put a cigarette anywhere and forget all about it. It was the regular smokers who were the careful ones." Joanna touched the ugly marks on the table. "That's why I'm so sure that this isn't Mum's work."

On Monday morning Joanna called to tell me that Fraser had returned to London with the Camps. He was not at all well. Would I go and see him? Not a professional visit, of course. Just to cheer him up. Fraser had not kept in touch with the people he'd known at school, and after an absence of ten years I was about the only friend he had in London.

I wasn't so sure that Fraser would think of me as a friend. When we'd first met, soon after his mother had married Dr Camp, I had been about six and he ten or eleven. At that time the difference in our ages had seemed huge. Even later, we'd had little to say to each other. It seemed to me that we hadn't talked to one another until he'd arrived from Australia for Joanna's wedding. He'd come to dinner at my house, with

Joanna and Jeremy, and he'd been interesting, but not in a personal way. By the end of the evening I'd still felt that I didn't know him. He didn't seem interested in people, except businessmen. Liz had said he was "all brains and no feelings". I rather thought that the failure to become friends with Joanna's brother had been mine. But he was Joanna's brother and that was a good enough reason for me to walk along to Baker Street shortly before noon.

Tubby opened the door and said Mrs Camp was out, so would I like to go straight up to Mr Fraser's room?

Fraser was in bed. He greeted me cheerfully, but I thought he didn't look at all well. The signs of jaundice could still be seen clearly. By now his skin shouldn't have been so yellow, and he was still looking weak. I guessed he'd lost more weight than he could afford.

"Norah, how long's this illness going to last?" he asked me.

"Jaundice doesn't disappear quickly."

"Some days I feel better. But I'm so weak. I'd like to go back to Australia. But then Mother would worry. . . . I'd meant to do quite a lot of work in England."

"Well, wait a little longer."

"How long? No, sorry, Norah, I don't expect you to answer me. You're not my doctor. The great Dr Camp's supposed to be in charge. Now tell me, what do you think of Joanna's flat?"

"It's attractive."

"But rather poor. I would like to do something for them, but I don't want to do the wrong thing. If I bought them a house, it would cost them far less than their flat. The London rents have become terrible. I thought I'd buy the house and have a flat in it for myself, which would allow me to pay the costs of running it. Do you think Joanna and Jeremy would accept that?"

"I think they'd like the idea of your having a home in their house. But why not just give them the money?"

"Joanna wouldn't accept it."

"I believe you're right. Wealthy people often are strange about money."

"But Joanna isn't wealthy. At twenty-one she received an income under the Petrie family trust. But inflation has halved the value of it. You see, our grandfather, who set up the trust, couldn't have guessed that that would happen."

"Couldn't you change the trust?"

"It would be extremely difficult while I'm alive. The company's wealthy, but the profits always have to go back into the business. So, you see, the family's personal wealth isn't as great as people might think. When my mother married Camp, most of her income had to go back to the company. That's why Aunt Theresa left her money to Mother."

"I'd have expected her to leave it to Joanna."

"So would I, though I can understand why Theresa did it. Joanna and Jeremy are young and clever and they're at the beginning of their working lives. Theresa must have felt that it was enough to give Joanna a generous wedding present and to leave her her personal things, such as jewellery. But Mother wouldn't have so much if she lost her husband. Besides, Theresa and Mother were very fond of each other. I'm sorry; this can't be very interesting to you, but I want to use you."

"How?"

"Prepare Joanna. I'm sure my plan would work if you told her that I intend to visit London more often, and that I'd like to have a place to stay in here. You'd prepare her better than me. One doesn't want to hurt Jeremy's pride."

"I'll do what I can." I got up. If I didn't hurry I would be late for everything for the rest of the day. Before my work at the surgery in the evening I had to see several patients in their homes.

"You'll come and see me again, Norah?"

"Of course. Anyhow, you'll soon be up again."

"One other thing. I need a solicitor. This jaundice has reminded me that I'm not going to live for ever."

"You want to make a will?"

"Don't sound so surprised, Norah. I'm probably the wealthiest member of the family."

I was about to leave the house when a door opened.

"Ah, Norah," Dr Camp greeted me. "Are you having lunch with us?"

"No, thanks, Dr Camp. I just wanted to say hullo to Fraser."

"That's kind of you."

His usually serious face lit up with a bright smile. When he was like this, one got the feeling that his hair must have turned white before it was time. He was looking almost youthful.

I suddenly wondered why I'd never used his Christian name, yet called his wife Joan. Of course, I hadn't seen as much of him. Perhaps, especially as a student, I'd felt too much respect for him because of his importance in the profession. But somehow neither reason quite explained my formality.

I said, "I'm sorry Fraser's making such slow progress."

"It is slow," he agreed. "Why not come down for a minute? I'd like to show you my new laboratory."

He took me down into a beautiful laboratory with the most modern equipment. It looked like a complete research laboratory.

"The one at my Nursing Home's always been too small for new work," said Dr Camp. "Now, at last, I have what I need."

"Wonderful," I said, and really meant it.

"Not bad, is it? And it has all the latest machinery, so that I don't need anyone to help me."

After I had looked around for some time, Dr Camp said, "I'm glad you've seen Fraser. What would you do with him?

I'd like your opinion."

"It's difficult to say, without seeing the results of full tests."

Dr Camp nodded. "I could see no reason for special tests until now. Fraser appeared to be getting better. Now — like you — I'm not happy about him. I think I'll have to move him to the Nursing Home, where we can do tests. I hope we don't find anything seriously wrong with him. It would finish my poor Joan."

"What is it that's affected her so much?" I asked. "Miss Petrie's death?"

"Partly. It did upset her badly. But you know, Norah, there's a far deeper problem. Though she doesn't seem to be, Joan's a very nervous person." He gave me that young attractive smile. "During the past years Joan's had several nervous breakdowns. They didn't last more than a few days, and they weren't serious. But lately she's become worse. Even Joanna's noticed it."

"May I ask what she does?"

"She smokes too much."

"I've noticed that too."

"And . . . I don't know what to call it. She's badly damaged pieces of furniture she used to be fond of. Norah, I'm telling you as a family friend, but I hope you won't repeat it; not even to Joanna and Fraser. As long as I can deal with Joan, there's no need to worry them. It wouldn't help Joan if they knew . . . but things have happened which have made me fear that there's something wrong with Joan's brain."

Five

"She'll see you if you come to the surgery tomorrow." Elsa was holding the telephone away from her ear. I could hear the voice at the other end of the line, fast and worried. "It's no use, Madame. I'm sorry, she's gone," Elsa lied. As she caught sight of me she looked uncomfortable. "No, you won't find her at home. She'll be out, visiting patients. Yes. Yes, I understand. I'll tell her."

"What was that about?" I asked.

Elsa came out from behind her desk. I didn't think she looked well; her face had the grey colour I'd noticed on other West Indians when they were sick. "It was a neighbour of mine, Doctor. Madame Taramova."

"Russian?"

"Sometimes Russian, sometimes Persian or Spanish. It all depends how she feels. She's funny, but I like her. She telephoned because she wants to be put on your list. She'd be on the Health Service, but she'd expect to be treated like a private patient, you know."

In our surgery we make no difference between private and Health Service patients who are really ill. When necessary we go to their homes, whoever they are.

"Madame Taramova wanted you to visit her. It's my fault, Doctor. I've been telling her about you — I mean, the way you look after your patients."

"Why did you tell her I wouldn't visit her?"

"There's nothing much wrong with her. It's all in her mind."

It annoys me when people who are not trained make judgements, but I couldn't be unkind to Elsa. If I'd criticised her she'd have worried about it for weeks after. "What do you know about Madame Taramova?"

"Well, she used to be a famous dancer. She's very old now, but she talks about working again. I don't think she'd be able to. She gets pains in her legs or her arms — different places. I go and see her because I feel sorry for her."

"Perhaps I *should* visit her."

"I don't know. She'll keep you there a very long time."

"She lives in your house?"

"No, Doctor, in the house next door to mine. She's in number seven, George Cottages."

"I was going to see Billy Corbett this evening, so I can visit your neighbour too. Afterwards you could give me a cup of tea. I'd like to see your new flat."

"Well. . . ." Elsa was doing some fast thinking. Then she smiled as brightly as she had before there'd been fear in her life. "That'll be nice, Doctor."

Billy was sitting on his bed by the window.

"Well, how are you getting on?" I said.

"I've been watching George Cottages. Only one man has gone into number five whom J.J. and his friends don't know about. I haven't told J.J. about Elsa. He thinks I watch people because I've got nothing else to do. Well, this man's been twice. I couldn't see his face properly because it was getting dark. He's tall — about one metre eighty-five. But not fat. He just looks strong. He wears American boots, and he's got dark hair . . . long, but not very long. Shorter than mine. That's not much, is it? What do you want me to do now, Doctor?"

"Keep watching, if you don't mind."

"Of course. I don't mind. What do you want me to look out for?"

"How often he comes. About what time. You might get some idea of his age."

"All right."

"And don't ask J.J. too many questions, Billy."

"All right. . . . Oh, there's something I forgot. You remember the man I was telling you about? Well, he stayed all night both times. Unfortunately I fell asleep at about six o'clock in the morning both times, so I never saw his face."

I suddenly realised just how hard it must be for one man to keep watch all night. "Billy, I don't want you to get so tired. You mustn't keep awake so many hours."

"Look, in football one gets used to watching attentively. It's a big part of the training and the game. So I can go on watching. I'm not very useful now, but that's something I can do. It's important as long as that dangerous man is there, isn't it?"

Madame Taramova's flat was full of pretty things from many parts of the world, and large numbers of signed photographs, but the furniture was cheap and poor.

Madame looked as strange as her home. She was wearing tight black clothing and a bright green cloak.

She apologised with some kind of foreign pronunciation for receiving me in her dancing clothes and for the state of her flat. She said she wasn't working just then, but that she'd been visiting agents — which took a lot of time.

"It is under the ground," she said, "but it is a very nice flat." She opened the two doors opposite the entrance to the living room. "Come, I will show you."

There was a very small kitchen, an even smaller bathroom and a bedroom.

"I even have a guest room with a shower. Well, it belongs to Mr Usher, the landlord, but if I want it for a friend he always says yes." She opened the door at the end of her bedroom. It led to a passage with an outside door and a small hall, through which we entered the guest room. It was entirely separate from Madame Taramova's flat, and it was clear that it had not been furnished by her. The brown armchairs, the carpet and the curtains looked expensive.

Madame Taramova led me back to her living room. "Mr

Usher is so kind. I have many, many friends who want to stay with me, and Mr Usher always says, 'You can have the guest bedroom, Madame.' It costs nothing extra. He understands it is a very hard life for a dancer. When I was with the Kirov Company. . . ."

Sitting at the table, I let her tell stories of her successes. Up to the neck, Madame's body would have been good enough for a forty-year-old woman, but the age of the head was not far from seventy.

At last she noticed that I'd been examining her.

"I'm very healthy — very strong," she told me. "But I need the doctors for my face. You see, I cannot afford my face any more."

"It's a nice face."

"Nice . . . nice," she said impatiently. "It's old. The agents say there is no work for a face like that. Oh, they're very nice, very polite. They all know my name. But no work. Doctor, you mustn't tell anyone."

"Elsa told me you have pains in your legs."

"I get pains when I'm unhappy — when I'm resting with no work to do. No, the only real pains are my face. Doctor, please, I want it lifted. That's what they call it, isn't it? Facelift. Can you arrange it? I would like it done on the National Health, please. It is for a professional purpose. Look!" She rose, got up on her toes and lifted her right leg. But I could see that she was unable to balance any longer. I felt sad.

I too got up, ready to catch her. "I'll find out whether it can be done," I promised. "But I'm sure there'll be a long waiting list for facelifts."

"It doesn't matter," she said cheerfully. "I'll wait. My mother — she was Russian — she was a hundred and four when she died."

Number seven George Cottages had been modernised with a lot of skill. Walking up the steps, I noticed the intelligent use that had been made of the space outside Madame

Taramova's front door. About half of Madame's yard was filled up by a tank for the house-heating oil supply and place for the rubbish. The whole of this was enclosed in a nice wall, partly hidden by climbing plants.

The flat roof of the box was only a metre below a window of the ground floor flat. There was even room for two or three garden chairs on it. Madame's entrance and the door to the little guest room had flower boxes full of pretty flowers on both sides.

I walked along the backs of several houses, turned left at the corner and left again to the front of George Cottages.

Elsa's ground floor flat, at the back of the hall at number five, was certainly very cheap. She'd told me that her rent, including central heating, was eight pounds a week. For this very low price she had quite a big living room, a bedroom, a small but useful kitchen and a bathroom.

I doubted whether any local house agent would have let such a flat to a West Indian with a job like Elsa's. The fact that Singh was a doctor had probably been the important thing.

Elsa showed me her home and then made tea. I asked her whether she liked her neighbours.

"They don't trouble me," she said, "and I pay no attention to them. Except Madame Taramova next door. She spoke to me the first time I came here. And the day I moved in she made a meal for Singh and me."

"Have you any news of Singh?"

"He's working at St George's Hospital. But I haven't heard from him. I'm not expecting anything."

I said, "I wish you'd let me help."

Elsa shook her head. "It's no use, Doctor. Look, my neck's healed up." Healed, yes. But the place still looked raw, and her face was thin and unhappy. "So . . . who cares!"

"I care. About you and someone else who got hurt. You aren't the only West Indian girl in Paddington who's been attacked."

"You shouldn't have talked."

"Someone talked to me. I know plenty of people in this district, as you know." I was certainly not going to mention Inspector Barrington. "The attack was so cruel that the girl almost died."

"It's got nothing to do with me."

"That's not like you, Elsa. How would you feel if the next attack ended with someone being killed?"

"I can't speak about it." Tears came into her eyes. "Please, Doctor, don't say any more."

"You can't stop me thinking," I told her. "I want the answer to one question. I know that you're being blackmailed. Why? For what?"

"No — no." Elsa turned away.

"It can't be for money." I hated putting pressure on the girl. Yet, if ever she and others like her were to be safe, I had to make my point and leave in her mind a strong argument against protecting the man who had attacked her. "There are very few reasons for blackmail, Elsa. In your case, it can't be money, and it can't be power. I mean, it isn't in your power to help any man get — let's say — a high position. That leaves nothing but a sexual reason."

Elsa still wouldn't look at me.

"The man's forced you into a relationship you don't want. He's done you a lot of harm. Yet you're protecting him. That, in your case, must mean that he's controlling you through something even greater than fear for your own safety. What could that be?"

Elsa remained silent.

"I will find the answer."

"Don't try. Please, Doctor. I love working at your place, and I don't want to give up the job."

"If you did, it wouldn't solve your problem."

"Believe me, nothing can solve it."

"Elsa, think about what I've said."

I was about to leave when I heard the sound of a key being

put in a lock. It seemed very near. With Elsa just behind me, I went to the front door and opened it suddenly. There was no one in the hall. Then I noticed a door just beside Elsa's. It had a lock but no handle.

"What's in there?" I asked.

"Nothing." She hid her shaking hands behind her back.

"It must be there for some purpose."

"Electricity meters and. . . ."

Looking into her frightened eyes I knew that Elsa would die rather than tell me what was on the other side of that door.

Six

Joan Camp was in her sitting room. She was pleased to see me, asked me to stay for tea, but didn't stop what she was doing, breaking some beautiful flowers into pieces and throwing them away. The flowers looked and smelled fresh.

When Joan had finished, she picked up the basket and put it beside the door. Tubby came in with the tea, and Joan asked her to get rid of the rubbish.

"What a pity," said Tubby. "They only arrived this morning."

"She's right," said Joan. "I should have given them away. It's just that flowers like those are the only ones I really dislike. They remind me of the war."

The war? It worried me. Why should Joan destroy fresh flowers and blame a war that ended more than thirty years before? Was this the sort of thing Dr Camp had been talking about when he said he was afraid her brain was not all right?

I said, "Everyone's allowed to dislike a few things."

"I shouldn't allow myself to get annoyed about little things. Poor Leon, I'm sure his intentions are good."

"He sent you the flowers?"

She smiled. "Who but a husband would do it? Choosing the wrong presents for twenty years. Look at this." She looked at the table which had replaced the one I had seen in the attic. "It must have been hard to find anything more wrong for this room."

It was the first time I'd heard her criticise Dr Camp or refer to the furniture he'd bought her.

"Why keep it there?"

Joan suddenly looked tired. "Oh, what does it matter?"

"It used to matter. You made quite a study of old English furniture."

"A hobby."

"Wasn't it more? I remember the lecture you gave at the Drama School: how one can make a room look ugly or attractive by putting the same furniture at different angles. We learned a lot from you, Joanna and I. Why keep things you dislike? Why not put back the table that used to stand here?" I asked.

"I can't. I'm afraid it's ruined. Hopelessly. Someone left cigarettes burning on it."

"Who'd do such a thing in *your* house?"

"Me, according to my husband."

"I can't believe it."

"Neither can I . . . most of the time. But I suppose it's possible. The table was the first of my pieces that got damaged. It happened when I went to visit Fraser, soon after he went to Australia."

"Surely it means you weren't here."

"I don't know. Leon said I burnt the table before I left. It almost started a fire. I love Australia . . . I was excited about the trip and seeing Fraser. Probably Leon was right. I sometimes forget things. You know, I love my house-plants; but I forget to water them and then they die."

"If your plants get dry, doesn't Tubby water them for you?"

"Of course, if Leon doesn't get there first. He always seems to notice before she does. Then he gives them too much water and kills them. I don't blame him; he just doesn't understand plants. I'm just as bad in my smoking habits. I light cigarettes and then forget where I've put them."

"Only for a moment." There had been many times when I'd seen her hunt for a lighted cigarette. Whenever I had been there she'd always found it burning harmlessly in an ashtray.

"I *think* I'm being careful. But I wouldn't swear to it any longer, not after the damage we've had in this house. I'm probably getting old."

"No, Joan, you're only fifty."

"Leon wouldn't share your opinion of me."

I was glad of the cup of tea in my hand. I drank it slowly, giving myself time to think. Joan had made it easier for me to understand her marriage — which she'd never done before. Was it because she now recognised me as an adult, an equal? Or was it a sign of getting old? I'd noticed that in many of my older patients: the sudden desire to talk about personal feelings, and about themselves and their past.

I asked, "Where did you meet Dr Camp?"

"At our family doctor's house in Sydney," Joan answered. "He'd been working at a London hospital, but he hadn't been satisfied there so he'd gone to Australia."

Joan wasn't smoking now. Looking calm and happy, she was talking freely of the past she'd never mentioned in all the years I'd known her. She talked of her beautiful house above a Sydney beach, of her first husband and her loneliness after his death. "What Leon and I had shared was a feeling of loss. Though I had my children, I couldn't get used to life without Bill. And Leon — though he'd found the kind of job he'd wanted — missed England very much. I somehow understood how he felt. Until Joanna adopted him, he had no friends and did not show any desire to marry."

"He must have been about forty then."

"That's right. Ten years older than I, though no one would have guessed it. He was an attractive man. He still is, isn't he? His nurses and his women patients think so."

Now, with Joan's money Dr Camp had been able to become a doctor in the world's most expensive medical street.

"You have no regrets?" I asked.

Joan looked at me as if she'd only just realised whom she'd been talking to. "Regrets? Most things in life go right or wrong because one is the person one is. Norah, I'm terribly worried. Fraser's been taken to the Nursing Home. And Leon won't allow me to see him."

Seven

When I left Joan, I walked to the Nursing Home. The hall, with its fine oil paintings of London, gave one the feeling of entering a beautiful private house.

The lift was on the way down. It landed silently. As the doors opened, two men began to push out a trolley. The body on it was completely covered with a purple sheet. The trolley moved off silently. I went up to the third floor and looked at the list of patients' names. Fraser Petrie was in room ten. When I got there, the door of room eleven stood wide open. Two girls were taking the sheets off the bed.

One of them saw me. "Mr Chabrier . . ." she said, and didn't seem to know how to go on.

I said, "I know. You've lost a patient."

She was clearly glad I hadn't come to visit the dead Mr Chabrier.

"He was very nice. Rheumatic fever it was."

Clearly the girl didn't know much about medicine. I turned to Fraser's door.

"Mr Petrie's not allowed visitors," said a nurse.

"Why not?"

"Doctor's orders."

"It's all right," I said. "I *am* a doctor."

"Oh." The girl looked doubtful.

I didn't give her time for objections. I firmly walked into Fraser's room.

He was asleep. His skin was still yellow and there were dark rings around his eyes. He looked worse than when I'd seen him at the Camp's house. I examined the chart at the foot of his bed. Without giving the cause, it showed that he was indeed a very sick man. I stood looking at him and finally decided to let him sleep on.

I was still trying to work out the pattern of his illness when Joanna came in. The sight of Fraser worried her so much that she did not object when I took her by the arm and led her out.

She said, "Now I know why Father won't let us see him. He's worse, Norah, isn't he?"

The lift was coming up. It stopped at our floor and Dr Camp came out. He seemed surprised to see us; unpleasantly surprised, I thought.

"I've told you to stay away, Joanna," he said. "I don't want *you* to get ill too."

"Daddy, I've seen him."

"All right," Dr Camp put an arm round her shoulders. "All right, girl. You'd better come to my office, both of you."

We went down to the ground floor and went into Dr Camp's office.

"I've been keeping you and your mother away from Fraser for safety," he said to Joanna. "I was hoping I'd soon have good news for you. Now — well, what I was afraid of has happened."

He opened a file on his desk, took out a small piece of paper and handed it to me. It was a report from a famous laboratory near the Nursing Home. All it said was AUSTRALIAN ANTIGEN +ve, but it was enough for me.

"I'd hoped for a negative report. But it's positive. It shows that Fraser's suffering from what is commonly called Australian jaundice." Dr Camp's voice was gentle. "It's highly infectious, Joanna."

"Daddy, how dangerous is it? Tell me. Please."

"It's serious, I'm afraid. We can only hope. . . ."

"But Fraser's always been so healthy. And he came to England weeks before. . . ."

"Australian jaundice is not a disease which one can only get in Australia. It was given the name because it was first discovered in Australia, in 1967. The Australian antigen is found in patients with various diseases. Unfortunately, it's in healthy people that it causes a dangerous form of jaundice."

"Daddy, is Fraser going to die?"

"At the moment we just don't know. You'd better have the truth."

"Can't you do something?"

"Don't you think we're doing all we can? It isn't much, that's the trouble. There's no known treatment, as Norah will tell you. We're giving Fraser cortisone. It's not a cure. But with luck, it'll allow the disease to burn itself out. Joanna, you could help a lot."

She looked at him hopefully.

Dr Camp picked up the report, which I'd put down on his desk. "I've only just received this. Fraser shouldn't be visited by anyone but the medical staff. It's to reduce the risk of his catching anything else. On the other hand, visitors could be infected by him. Now, Joanna, I want you to tell your mother that you've seen Fraser — against my wishes; and that he's improving."

"How can I, Daddy?"

"I haven't finished. Explain to your mother that Fraser's getting medicine which will cure him, provided he doesn't get any infection from outside. It's important to make her understand why she — and you — mustn't see him yet."

"But what will happen if he dies? Mum would never forgive me for lying to her."

"Joanna, my dear, you must let me deal with this."

"I think we should tell Mum how ill Fraser is."

"If all goes well, she'll never know. It would be wrong to cause her unnecessary misery. Why don't you and Jeremy take her down to the cottage next week-end? Norah, perhaps you could go too. You young people and her garden will make her forget her troubles."

"Well, Mum might go with us. But she won't forget Fraser. She'll be thinking of him all the time."

"Not if you're clever. You're an actress, Joanna . . . a good one. For your mother's sake, play your part well. I know you can do it."

"I don't know whether I should."

"Won't you trust me?" Dr Camp said. "Haven't we always trusted each other?"

Joanna nodded.

"For a person who isn't a doctor this is hard to understand, I know. But I'm trying to protect Fraser, above all. The medicine we're giving him interferes with his natural resistance against diseases. Therefore we must do everything we can to keep such things away from him. And the most important way we can do that is to keep out all visitors . . . to make sure that no one, except essential medical staff, gets anywhere near him. Even your mother might pass something on to him that could kill him. That's why I want her kept away. Does this make sense, Jo?"

"Yes, Daddy."

"Then you'll do as I ask?"

"I'll try."

Of course Joanna persuaded her mother to leave London, and Dick Markham agreed to exchange duty week-ends with me. Liz, who had to meet someone in Oxford, couldn't come to Sussex with us.

We left on Saturday, soon after lunch, in Joanna's car, driven by Jeremy. In spite of the heavy traffic out of London we got to Southdown Village in two hours.

The Camps' country place had once been a row of four farm-workers' cottages. An earlier owner had joined them into one house and bought extra land, so that it now had quite a big garden. Later Joan had turned the stables into a self-contained cottage for Aunt Theresa.

We had tea outside, enjoying the hot sun and the bright colours of the huge tree at the back of the cottage. Afterwards we played tennis.

At about six Jeremy suggested a drink at the Crown. Joan said she'd cook the dinner and sent us off on our own. We didn't feel guilty about leaving her behind. Though she left the daily cooking in London to Tubby, she enjoyed making a meal for a party in the country.

The bar at the back of the Crown Hotel, which the village people used, was crowded. We were greeted by Farmer Tachbrook and by Mr and Mrs Bray, who grew vegetables to sell in the market. We were made to feel at home, probably because of Joanna, who was generally considered the most famous Southdown Villager. Hadn't she begun her acting as a child in the village hall plays? Tachbrook told us about his good farming season and complained about the rising price of feeding stuffs. The Brays talked about the village's fight against council plans for widening the road into Southdown Village.

News of Joanna's presence must have got to the Manager. He appeared with Washington as Jeremy was ordering more drinks, and refused to let us pay for them.

Washington was a big strong eighteen-year-old who was not quite an idiot, but almost. No one knew who his parents were. He'd been found when he was a few days old, in a garden in the village of Washington. Mr and Mrs Masters, who had no children of their own, had looked after him, and he'd been with them ever since. They'd given him a name, but no one had ever used it: from the beginning, the people of Southdown Village had called him Washington. Although his brain was so poor, the boy was earning a living working with Mr Masters.

The only thing he did well on his own was dealing with animals. He had a natural understanding of them, knowing how to take care of sick dogs, birds with damaged wings and lost cats. After Miss Theresa's death, Joan had allowed him to keep Theresa's old cat, Pekoe, and he'd looked after her ever since. She had even come to the hotel with Washington.

While Masters was discussing with Joanna and Jeremy his plans for moving into Miss Theresa's cottage, the Manager was talking to me about the old lady's death.

"It was a shock to the whole village, Doctor. She had never complained about her health. Half an hour before she died I saw her eating fish salad, and the next moment — well, it seemed like a moment — Dr Camp was calling down from Miss Joanna's room. . . ."

"Joanna's room?" I said.

"Yes, we'd given it to her to change in after the wedding ceremony. In the end . . . well, we had to put her things into another bedroom. It all happened so fast."

I suddenly realised that there was a time immediately before Miss Theresa died of which I knew nothing. I'd collected the information which was needed for filling in the cremation certificate, but as the Manager had not been present at the death, I'd asked him no questions.

"Miss Theresa was at the party half an hour before she died?"

Mr Smythe nodded.

"And then?" I asked.

"The next thing I knew," he said, "was that our telephone

girl came rushing into the kitchen. She said Dr Camp had telephoned from the bride's room. He wanted me to go up. I went at once. When I got to number five, I just couldn't believe it. I mean, the doctor's bag and stethoscope. . . ."

I'd forgotten the stethoscope. When I had entered the room it had still been on Dr Camp's neck. "The doctor must have been listening to Miss Theresa's heart. After that he gave her an injection, didn't he?"

"I don't know. By the time I got there it was all finished. Though I did see a syringe on the dressing table and those broken — I don't know what they're called. . . ."

"Ampoules."

"Ah, yes, the ampoules. They contain the stuff that goes into syringes, don't they? I remember during the war we used to be given injections before we were sent abroad. It was a funny thing: there was a captain — a big man — who hated injections. He fainted every time. Would you believe it? But he was a very brave man in a battle. When we were in the Western Desert. . . ."

It was as if he was telling me the stories of films; they didn't seem real. And yet it wasn't long ago that I'd seen the battles of Vietnam on television. Did one have to smell violence before one's brain could fully understand how terrible war was?

Something in what Mr Smythe had said worried me, but I could not think what it was.

As we were going out through the crowd, the cat came down from Washington's shoulder and went to the door with us. Joanna picked her up. "Go back, Pekoe . . . back to sleep."

Washington took the cat. "She doesn't forget," he said. "Pekoe knew Miss Theresa was coming. . . ."

"Now, boy!" Masters said. "We don't want any of that. Miss Theresa's gone away," he added more gently. "That's why Pekoe's yours now."

"Pekoe knew, Daddy — as I've been telling. . . ."

"Stop it. Do you hear? And say good-night."

"Nights." Washington held the cat with both hands — as if to protect it. "Always nights." He was looking past Joanna through the open door, and seemed extremely frightened.

The people in the bar were used to Washington. In a kind way, they'd always laughed at his strange ideas, and he had laughed with them. Not now. Like me, they'd seen the terrible fear in the poor boy's eyes. They'd become silent, and some of them were looking uncomfortable.

After tennis, beer at the Crown and a big dinner we all felt sleepy.

By the time I'd had a shower Joanna was in bed. I noticed that her room looked bright. The door of the cupboard had been replaced by a long mirror which reflected the bed and the trees beyond the window.

"What do you think of it?" asked Joanna.

"Good idea."

"Even better in daylight. Now we can lie in bed and watch Tachbrook's cows in the mirror. Press the button on the right, Norah."

I did. The mirror slid slowly sideways until the cupboard behind was completely open.

"Daddy made it, electric wires and all."

"Since when's your father been good at making things?"

"You're right, Norah; he doesn't often have time for it. But when I was small, in Australia, he invented the most wonderful toys for me. He always seemed to know what I'd like, even before *I* did. My real father couldn't have been more wonderful. And now this mirror."

"So that's why he wanted you to go to the cottage this week-end."

"Well, he'd planned it as a surprise." Joanna gave me a card with a loving message from her father. "But I'm sure he was more anxious to give Mum a holiday. In London she's too near the Nursing Home. You know, Norah, I've been thinking and thinking about it. Daddy's taken an awful lot upon himself. He's made me tell Mum lies about Fraser's condition, to stop her worrying and to make her feel it was safe for her to go away. And that must be good for Mum. But if Fraser got worse. . . ."

"He'd telephone you."

"Mum's been trying to telephone Daddy. There was no answer. And he wasn't at the Nursing Home. The nurse said Fraser was 'comfortable' — whatever that means. I'm worried. Why had Daddy disappeared? He's always at home on Saturday nights."

"He must get an emergency call occasionally."

"When he does, he sends out one of the doctors from the Nursing Home. He's been doing that for the past ten years."

"I wouldn't have thought that your father had such fixed habits."

"That shows that you don't really know him. But then, few people do — outside the family."

"I'd believe you if I hadn't read his articles in medical magazines. He's been doing advanced research work. And people who do such work must be imaginative, they're rarely people with fixed habits."

"That sounds reasonable, Norah. But it's no good talking about Daddy like that, because there's no one else like him in the world."

"All right. You win." Looking at Joanna, with her soft black hair and those clear grey eyes, one had to let her win. In her own way, she probably did know best. I had a real respect for her insight.

"I wish I knew what's happening. Daddy shouldn't be out tonight. He shouldn't be: I know it."

Eight

The first time I woke that night was just before two in the morning. The curtains were moving in the wind. Suddenly I heard it — a strange sound. If it had been daytime, I'd have said that someone was sawing wood. At night it was unlikely. The sounds – soft and yet clear – seemed to come from the side of the cottage where Miss Theresa's room had been.

Perhaps it was Washington, I thought. Perhaps he really was mad.

Before I fell asleep again I heard the church clock strike two.

I felt I hadn't been asleep more than a few minutes when I woke again. This time I thought I heard footsteps — soft and regular, as if the person was wearing heavy rubber boots. Washington? Who else? I pulled the blankets over my ears.

When I woke again the birds had begun to sing, and a cock was shouting. But there was another sound, much closer; opposite our room. It was as if someone was slowly and cautiously opening a door.

This time, wondering whether Joan was feeling ill, I got up and went out into the passage. No one was there. But I saw the door of the children's bathroom move from the half-open to the almost closed position.

I went across, opened it and put on the light. Of course the bathroom was empty. I firmly shut the door and went back to bed.

The morning was so fresh and sunny that I forgot the disturbed night. After breakfast we all went for a walk.

On the way home — with Joan and Joanna a long way behind, Jeremy and I talked about Fraser.

"Norah, is he as ill as Joanna thinks?" asked Jeremy.

"I'm afraid so."

We walked on in silence.

At last Jeremy asked, "Shouldn't we get a specialist to see him?"

"I don't think it would help. Dr Camp's had a laboratory report. I've seen it. It proves that Fraser has Australian jaundice."

"Poor Joanna. She's been so happy about her brother's proposal. She's been looking forward to us living with Fraser."

"When Fraser mentioned the idea to me, he was afraid Joanna and you wouldn't be happy about it."

"Well, he knows better now. Joanna would agree to anything that brings him closer. I had no brother or sisters, so I can understand how she feels."

"You like Fraser?"

"Very much."

"He isn't easy to get to know."

"Shy, sensitive people rarely are. . . . Norah, isn't there *something* more we can do for Fraser? It could be that Dr Camp is too close to it all. If there's anything you can think of . . . anything at all. . . ."

That night I woke suddenly again. I don't know why. It was in this silence that I heard a sound that filled me with fear — something like a scream. Immediately after, a door shut suddenly.

I got up and put on the light in the passage. Joan was standing outside her room, leaning against the door, as if she was trying to stop someone from getting out. I could see that she was extremely nervous.

"You did hear it too, didn't you?" she said to me. She was making an obvious effort to make it sound normal.

"Yes, Joan. An animal, I suppose. It's a pity it woke you up."

"There have been other . . . strange noises. Norah, could I possibly be imagining it all?" It seemed to me that she was afraid of her own fears.

"If you mean the sawing, Joan. . . ."

"Yes," she said eagerly. "Yes, last night."

"I heard it too, and the noise of the bathroom door. There are simple explanations for them all. I think it's Washington. He's probably wandering around."

"And screaming?"

"That must have been an animal."

Joan shook her head. "No, it was different. I'm used to natural sounds."

I had an idea. "Couldn't it have been Pekoe? Some cats can sound almost human."

"I don't know." Joan seemed almost ready to accept my idea.

"I'll go down."

"No, Norah. There's no need. I'm all right. Really. It must have been Pekoe."

"Let me make you a hot drink."

She came away from the door and touched my hair. "You're a sweet girl, Norah. But you don't have to worry about me. I'm not exactly a lion, but I'm not a mouse either. I'm going to take a sleeping tablet and go straight back to bed."

I woke up several times during the rest of the night, and got up early, glad to see the daylight.

I dressed and went down to the kitchen. I put on the coffee pot and went out, round the house. It was a grey morning but the sun was trying to break through. I walked across the garden, enjoying the shape of the old trees under the hills.

It was after I'd turned back — intending to stop the coffee from boiling over — that the big tree in the middle of the garden caught my attention. I stopped. Suddenly I wondered whether I was awake, whether I wasn't still in bed dreaming. There was something about the tree that looked as strange as any of my worst dreams. Pekoe, the cat, was sitting quietly on a branch, about four metres from the ground. She was beside a piece of rope. And from the rope hung a body. The dead body of Washington.

Nine

The police were helpful and sympathetic. They examined the buildings and garden carefully and were sure that Washington had killed himself. The police doctor and I agreed.

It was Masters who provided the information which gave a reason for the suicide. Washington, he said, had never gone out at night until the previous Sunday. That night he'd disappeared. But it hadn't been until three in the morning that Mr and Mrs Masters had discovered it. They'd found him at last, hiding under the stairs. He was terribly frightened. They'd helped him to go back to bed, and Mrs Masters had stayed with him until the morning.

Though Washington hadn't been able to tell them what had upset him, he had mentioned Miss Theresa several times, and that had given them an idea. The old cat which had normally slept on the boy's bed must have visited her old home. As Pekoe rarely left the house at night, Washington must have gone to look for her at the cottage.

Masters couldn't say what might have frightened Washington, but he believed that he'd seen or heard something strange. Washington had mentioned Miss Theresa as if she were still at her cottage. He'd said that Pekoe knew! He'd always been a cheerful boy, but now he had become unhappy when it got dark, and he had watched

Pekoe as if he was afraid that someone would seize the cat and take it away from him.

If pure fear had driven Washington to suicide, how was it that someone with as weak a brain as he had had succeeded in killing himself? Masters said that the boy had liked watching television. He had seen people hanging themselves there; and unfortunately the rope had been easy to find: it had been round a piece of ground that Washington himself had put grass seed on.

At midday Washington was taken away. The police said they'd have to arrange an inquest for Wednesday, when I could most easily attend.

If there was any mystery in Washington's suicide, it appeared to have been in the boy's confused mind. The police, Joan, Joanna, Jeremy and I explained everything else. The picture we'd built up between us should have satisfied me. And yet, it didn't.

Liz had arrived home before me. She had made some bread and prepared a beautiful dinner. She told me about her week-end and her friends at Oxford University, and we'd almost finished the meal before I could tell her about Washington.

"Poor thing. It's strange . . ." she said thoughtfully. "He seemed so happy. In a way, happier than normal people. Are you sure he killed himself?"

"No doubt."

"It's funny. I'd *thought* you'd have a difficult week-end, with Joan worrying about Fraser but not this. Things have been happening to the Camps ever since Joanna's wedding. Fraser getting ill. Miss Theresa dying in the middle of the reception. And now Washington. All in one month. As if there were a curse on them."

"Well," I said, "let's hope that's the end of it. Now, will you please let me have the messages."

Liz went to the study and returned with a piece of paper. "The Russian woman telephoned — the one who wants a facelift."

"What do you know about that?"

"She told me." Liz laughed. "She said you were arranging it. Are you?"

"That's none of your business. What did she want?"

"Just letting you know that Elsa's got a bad cold and won't be at the surgery. Madame — I can't read the name. . . ."

"Taramova."

"Right. She's looking after Elsa."

When I went to see Billy the next day, J.J. was just coming out of the block of flats. "Good evening, Doctor. Are you visiting our boy? He's all right. He won fifty pounds tonight."

"What have you been doing, J.J.?"

"Me? Nothing. Just did a bit of gambling — for Billy."

It was Saturday evening again, and a lot of people were gambling in the street.

"Take my advice, Doctor. Go and do some gambling. Go to Ted. He's honest. Tell him I sent you."

"Thank you, J.J., but I always lose when I gamble. I've got to earn my living. And don't teach Billy such things."

"Of course not, Doctor! Well, good-night then. Don't forget. If you want to try the cards, go to Ted."

When I went in to see Billy, he told me that the man had been to Elsa's house again . . . and that he had left just after midnight.

He said, "I call him American Boots. He always wears them. He didn't stay as long as usual last Saturday. How's Elsa?"

"Off work. She's got a cold."

"He hasn't been doing things to her again?"

"I don't think so. A neighbour's looking after her."

"The old dancer?"

"That's right."

"I'll tell you one thing, Doctor. American Boots isn't young. I thought he was in his twenties, but he could be forty."

"How do you know, Billy?"

"I noticed the way he walks. In football you get to know the difference: the young players and the older ones don't move in the same way."

At Elsa's, Madame Taramova opened the door."Doctor, it is kind of you to come." She took me into the living room. "Elsa is not well. Yesterday she came for lunch. Before she ate, her face went grey — you know the colour that West Indians can be. Then she nearly fainted. I made her eat her soup. Then I took her home. She didn't have much fever yesterday, but now it is 39.5°."

Elsa was lying flat on her back. Her eyes opened. "Doctor . . . I'm sorry I didn't come to work."

"That's all right. Are your arms and legs aching?"

"Yes. It's flu, isn't it?"

"Let's see your throat."

She let me examine her as if she didn't care what was wrong. It probably was flu. At this stage one couldn't be sure.

Back in the living room Madame Taramova said, "Doctor, Elsa is so sad. It is not right for a young girl." She pointed towards the medical books on the table. "She loves the young doctor very much. It is wrong for him to leave her."

"Has she told you why they broke off their engagement?"

"No. But she speaks of Dr Singh — what he used to like or not like. I wish he knew she was sad."

The old lady and I left the flat together. Elsa had given her a key; Madame Taramova had promised to return in the morning. She said good-night, and was about to turn the corner into her road when I noticed the back of a tall man. He completely fitted Billy's description.

"Ah, Mr Usher." Madame Taramova had also seen him. "He is back."

"The man with the American boots?"

"No, Mr Usher is Canadian. He is very kind. He lends me

his rooms for my guests. I have so many friends. . . ."

So "American Boots" was not, as Billy believed, a person who had no business at George Cottages. Though his rooms were in Madame Taramova's road, the front of the house was next door to Elsa's. Perhaps Billy had been mistaken in thinking that he'd been entering Elsa's house.

What puzzled me was Mr Usher's arrangement with Madame Taramova. How could the Canadian lend her his room when he clearly kept on using it himself?

I said, "It's good of you to look after Elsa when you're so busy with your guests."

"There is a lot of time." She watched the Canadian walk into a shop. "These days my friends do not stay so much."

These days, I suddenly realised, there were no visitors — except in the old dancer's mind.

Ten

As I put a culture bottle into my bag the next morning, I had no clear idea what I wanted it for. But by the time I saw Elsa, I knew that I had to find out the exact cause of her fever. I'd expected her temperature to be down this morning, yet I wasn't surprised when I found it hadn't changed. It was still 39.5°.

She spoke and moved in a slow, tired way until she saw me take a syringe out of my bag. And then she suddenly sat up, looking obviously frightened.

"I don't want an injection. I don't want it. Don't put a needle in me."

"Elsa, listen. I'm not giving you an injection. I just want a little of your blood."

"I don't want it," she cried. "I don't."

"I promise you it won't hurt. You won't feel it. Look," I showed her the culture bottle. "I want to put your blood in there. You know about cultures, don't you? I'll take the bottle to the hospital laboratory. And in two or three days the culture will have grown and we'll know what's making you feel so ill. Then I'll be able to give you the right treatment, without having to guess. All right?"

She was still looking suspicious. "Doctor, you're not just saying it? You're not going to put something into me?"

"Of course not. You can watch." I held up the syringe. "It's empty, isn't it? You can see."

"All right," she agreed.

I took the blood from her arm. Afterwards one could hardly see the mark at all. "I'm going to give you penicillin, Elsa."

"I don't want injections."

"You'll be taking tablets. You don't mind that, do you?"

"No."

"You will take the tablets, won't you?"

"Yes, Doctor. I want to get back to work."

"Has anyone been visiting you?"

She shook her head. "No." She knew what I'd meant. "Only Madame Taramova. When can I go back to work?"

"We'll wait for a day or two."

"You won't tell anyone?"

"Tell what, Elsa?"

"The result of the blood test . . . whatever it is. I don't want anyone to know."

"That's silly. I don't talk to other people about my patients."

"No. I'm sorry."

Suddenly I thought of a new possibility. Clearly Elsa had become mixed up with a man whose brain was not working properly. Was he like that because he was taking drugs? Had he made Elsa take drugs? And was Elsa, who wouldn't know what one could find in a culture and what one couldn't, afraid that I'd discover it?

Whatever was causing Elsa's fever, she was afraid as well as ill. Some fear had wiped out the cheerful behaviour which had made her popular with all of us at the surgery. Looking at the expression on her face, I gave up hope that she'd ever tell me what was happening to her. I'd have to find out on my own.

I left George Cottages with the uncomfortable feeling that I should have acted sooner.

I was waiting in St George's Hospital while an Indonesian nurse was trying to find Dr Singh Awar for me.

I remembered what Camp had said about the Asians and Africans in Britain. He belonged to an age in which the English had been the top people in the world. I had never made comparisons between races, because I was younger. But unfortunately people like Dr Camp still influenced the behaviour of people of my age. Because so many of the older people still did not treat nurses from the West Indies or South East Asia and doctors from India or Pakistan with respect, people of my age tried to be especially polite to them.

By the time Dr Singh Awar arrived, I knew how not to behave.

I asked, "Have I come at a bad time, Singh?"

"Not at all. What can I do for you . . . Norah?"

It seemed a good beginning that he'd called me by my first name too. "Is there anywhere we can talk privately?"

Singh went and opened a door opposite. "This office is empty. Come in. It's difficult to find a quiet corner." He pulled out a chair for me and himself sat on the desk.

I said, "Elsa's far from well."

There was interest in Singh's dark, intelligent eyes. And then he looked away. "I'm sorry." Minutes seemed to pass before he spoke again. "What's the matter with her?"

"At the moment, it looks like flu. But that's not the most worrying thing. About three weeks ago Elsa was attacked." Singh was really upset now.

I told him of the nasty wound on Elsa's neck, of her refusal to speak of the person who'd hurt her and of her general state of depression and fear. "I'm certain that she's being made to do things against her will."

"Against her will. . . ." Singh looked at me as if I'd brought him good news. "Yes . . . it must have been. You're sure?"

"I am, though I have no proof. That's why I've come to see you."

"You want to know why our engagement ended?"

"It might help."

"It wasn't my fault. I didn't want to lose Elsa. I'd lost my home and my country. I'll never be able to return to Uganda. With Elsa I could see my future in England. A family of my own. There was no doubt in my mind that Elsa was the girl I wanted for my wife. It was she who suddenly changed."

"When did it happen?"

"A day or two after she'd moved into the new flat. I went there . . . it was about ten at night. She'd never drunk or smoked, she used to dislike the smell of cigarettes. But that evening she smelled of alcohol, and the room was full of smoke. She told me to get out."

"Just like that?"

Singh nodded. "I tried to argue with her. I said she was drunk."

"Was she?"

"I don't think so. I was certain that she had someone in the flat. I opened the bedroom door. She stopped me going in . . . she kicked and screamed. It was terrible."

"Did you see anyone?"

"Yes. Not clearly. He was in bed, and there wasn't much light. He was a white man with long dark hair. He wore sunglasses. Perhaps I shouldn't have rushed out. But I didn't want to do anything stupid."

"Was that the last you saw of Elsa?"

"No, I went back a few days later. I thought she'd tell me . . . I don't know what. I was ready to believe her, to accept any excuse. But she said she no longer loved me. She gave me back the engagement ring. There was nothing I could do. You say she's been forced to. . . ."

"She's terribly afraid of the man."

"That's about the only explanation that makes sense to me. Norah, what do you suggest?"

"Your description of the man may be helpful." I was very conscious of the fact that the description would fit a number of men other than Madame Taramova's landlord and the person Billy had watched through his binoculars. But now, for the first time, I could be sure that Elsa was mixed up with a European with long hair.

"Shall I go to her, Norah?"

"I hoped you'd be willing. But would you mind if I first talked with my friend in the police? What we need is something — a little bit of knowledge about him — to make her see that she's ruining her life for nothing. But if she's going to talk at all, it will be to you."

"So you want me to wait?"

"If you agree that it might be wise. You'd have a better chance of getting her to talk if we had some more information; if we could at least guess her reasons for protecting the person who attacked her."

"I agree. You'll let me know when I can go to see her?"

"Of course, Singh. I'm glad you still love Elsa."

"One doesn't love a woman for what one wishes her to be, but for what she is. I'm happy to know that she isn't guilty of anything."

"I believe she isn't, but I don't know."

"If you hadn't come to me," said Inspector Barrington, "I'd

have visited you this evening."

We were in his office.

Inspector Barrington opened the file he had put between us and took out the photograph of a man. "Does this mean anything to you, Doctor?"

"Aged about forty. Irish."

Barrington smiled, "Irish, unemployed and impossible to employ. You haven't met the gentleman?"

"No."

"It's a pity. It would have been useful if he'd been a patient of yours." He put the picture back in the file. "Paddy's a psychopath, I'm told. He appeared in our area about fifteen years ago. He went to prison for robbery with violence; then he kept out of trouble for two years, but after that he got worse and was in prison again for violence. I wish they'd kept him there. But of course he was let out and we had a lot of trouble finding him again. Now we've arrested him for attacking a girl in Praed Street. He's confessed to other crimes of the same kind — including attacks on coloured girls. You may tell your young nurse that Paddy's locked up. It should make her feel safer."

"Thank you, Inspector. Only — I don't think he's the man who attacked Elsa."

"Oh? How's that?"

"I've had a description of him from people I can trust and it isn't like your picture of Paddy."

"Not again!" Barrington groaned. "You've been doing our job for us. And I thought you'd learned your lesson when you almost got yourself killed last year. . . . Oh, very well," he saw that I was going to object. "It was a medical puzzle and you prevented something terrible happening. But this is different, Dr North. We are dealing with a criminal."

"Are we, Inspector? You've just told me that Paddy is a psychopath."

"And you say that Paddy's not the right man."

"According to Dr Singh Awar, he isn't. On the other

hand, the person Dr Awar described — as far as he could see him — also happens to have a brain which is disturbed."

"And you think that that gives you the right to interfere?"

"It makes it necessary for me to do so." I was not very happy; the Inspector was getting annoyed with me. If I was to get what I'd come for, I'd have to change his feelings towards me; completely. "Believe me, I have no desire to do your job for you. But even if Elsa were a stranger, I'd have to pay attention to her health problems. And I'd have to try to solve them."

"All right, Dr North, I can't stop you keeping your eyes open. There've been times when I wished I could, but just don't try to stop a bus with your nose. I'd hate to have our next meeting at the hospital with you dead. And now you'd better tell me what you want. I don't think you're paying me a social visit."

"I'd like to meet the other West Indian girl who was attacked."

He told me that her name was Aureol, and gave me her address in a poor part of East London.

I drove there, and began looking for the place where Aureol Dunn lived. The people who were hurrying through the rain reminded me again of Dr Camp's dislike of our changed population. Without exception, they were West Indian or African.

The first person I met in Aureol's house was a man in his twenties, who came out of one of the rooms. When I asked for Aureol Dunn, he looked at me angrily.

"I'm a doctor," I said.

"Oh?" His expression didn't change. "Has she asked you to come?"

"Ask her."

"All right. Number fourteen, second floor."

For a moment I expected him to follow me upstairs, but he continued along the passage, out of the house.

I had to bang on the door of number fourteen to make myself heard above the loud sound of voices and a radio. At last an old man opened the door. Yes, he said, Aureol was in. He left me standing outside, and made his way across the room, which was crowded with a dozen people sitting on beds and children playing about the floor. The girl he spoke to came out into the passage and shut the door behind her.

"What do you want?" She was tall and would have been pretty if half her face hadn't been cut in two by a scar between the corner of her mouth and her ear.

I told her about Elsa. I begged her for the information which the police needed if further attacks on girls were to be prevented. Whilst she listened to me, I thought that she felt sympathy for Elsa. But as soon as I asked a direct question about the man who had attacked her, Aureol's face changed.

"I remember nothing," she said. "I've been ill."

"I know you've been ill. You've had a bad time; that's why you'd understand better than anyone how Elsa. . . ."

"Why don't you ask *her* about the man?" Aureol interrupted. "Why come to me? If she isn't saying anything, that's her problem."

"She isn't well enough."

"That devil — him and his dirty engineering!"

"Engineering? What do you mean?"

"Forget it." Aureol had already calmed down again. "If you know what's good for you, keep away from him. And don't come here asking questions. I've had enough."

"Wait!" I managed to get between her and the door. "Think it over. We must find the man before he kills someone. Don't be afraid; the police will keep your name out of it."

"I don't remember anything," Aureol repeated.

"Here's my address." I held out a card. "Telephone me if you change your mind."

She took the card and put it in her pocket.

When I got back home, my sister was waiting for me.

"Joan Camp's been here," Liz said.

I'd smelled the cigarette smoke.

"She wanted to see you. She looked ill. Dr Camp says that Fraser's getting better. But I think Joan doesn't believe he's going to live."

I drove down to Sussex for the inquest. It took less than an hour.

Everyone agreed that it was impossible to be sure what had been going on in Washington's simple mind, or what had brought fear and suicide into his quiet little world.

At eight-thirty the next morning the telephone woke me. It was Dr Paul from the laboratory at St Mary's Hospital.

"Norah, I've got the result of Miss Elsa Barbuda's blood-culture," he said. "Your patient hasn't got common flu. Your guess was a clever one."

A clever guess? Oh, no, a subconscious one. Having a blood-culture done for a patient with flu was not usual. That's why I'd gone to Dr Paul personally. Yet I couldn't pretend to myself that the result didn't surprise me. It did.

As I thanked Dr Paul, my brain began to work at double speed. A whole mass of little things — forgotten bits of knowledge — fell into place, making me realise how stupid and blind I'd been. If I'd paid more attention to Billy, or even to my own sister, I'd have known weeks ago who the man was who'd attacked Elsa and almost killed Aureol. I'd have to move cautiously, but fast, if I was to prevent him from killing the next girl he found.

Eleven

Elsa was feeling neither better nor worse. No doubt the penicillin had helped. When I explained what kind of infection she had and told her that she should be able to return to work in a couple of weeks, she looked less depressed.

Madame Taramova promised to make sure that Elsa took the new medicine I wanted her to take.

"Her body will recover," said Madame Taramova. "But it is her broken heart that is the trouble."

"Because of your kindness she isn't alone."

"It is nothing. Elsa is a sweet girl . . . she might have been my daughter. I'll sleep in Elsa's living room until the fever is over. Is that long enough?"

"More than enough, Madame Taramova."

"I've told my friends they cannot come to stay with me for some time, because I'm nursing my young neighbour. They're very good friends, so they understand."

"I'm arranging for you to see someone about your facelift. You should get an appointment in two or three weeks."

"Ah, that will be wonderful. When I have the new face. . . ."

"You'll have to wait for an operation, I'm afraid."

"How long, Doctor?"

"It could be as long as three or four years, if you want a facelift under the National Health Service."

"It doesn't matter. I have time. My mother, who was Russian, lived until she was a hundred and four."

"When I spoke to Fraser on the telephone this morning he sounded terribly weak," Joan said. She was walking up and down in her sitting room, smoking a cigarette.

I said, "He's been seriously ill."

"Norah, I believe he's worse."

"What's your husband saying?"

"That Fraser's getting better. I wish I could see the boy! Oh, I know; Leon's explained that it's safer for Fraser if I don't, but. . . ."

"He's also thinking of you. Australian jaundice is dangerous."

"Doctors and nurses see him."

"They have to do so, and they're used to taking care."

"I have a feeling that there's something I should be doing for Fraser; but I don't know what. It's true, Fraser's in a very good private nursing home, being treated by a very good doctor. Yet, there's this strange thought I have. . . . Norah, am I being silly? Joanna doesn't think so."

"Neither do I."

"I want the truth, but Leon never has time to discuss things with me."

"Would you like me to speak with him?"

"Yes, I think so."

"Could I see his appointments book?"

"That's a good idea. It's not always easy to find Leon."

I followed Joan across the hall, down to the laboratory. There was no one there, yet the place had a curious life of its own. Small lights were switching on and off and the sounds the switches made made me feel that Dr Camp was about to appear from behind the rows of growing cultures.

We found his appointments book in the office, beside the telephone. Joan looked through the week's jobs. "Just look at it. It isn't surprising that he gets so tired."

"What about Saturday?" I asked. "He has nothing down for tomorrow."

"All the same, he'll be out," said Joan. "On Saturdays we used to go to the cottage or have guests here — as you know. But that's changed. Leon says he's got to spend more time at the hospital. He blames the lack of British doctors in hospitals. Most of the lower ones are foreigners, and Leon won't trust them. He thinks the training at certain foreign medical schools is too poor. So he has to do more himself. For the first time, even the Nursing Home's had to employ a Pakistani doctor. He's not complaining about Dr Mosin. But you know how he feels about coloured people."

"This is another thing I don't understand." Joan was listening to the quiet sounds of the laboratory. "All these machines. He had to have them. What for? Ever since we returned from Australia he's been using hospital laboratories. They seemed to satisfy him. Now, almost at the end of his working life, this private laboratory. Why?"

I went to the Nursing Home at noon, and there was neither a doctor nor a nurse in sight. I had chosen this time because the medical staff would have finished their morning's work, so that the patients could have lunch.

As I'd expected, none of the servants paid any attention to me. They were so used to people in white medical coats that they hardly even saw me. I went to Fraser's room and looked at him through the glass in the door.

I was shocked by his appearance. Within the past week he'd lost more weight than he could afford, and his skin had turned from yellow to white. There was no doubt — he was more dead than alive.

I hurried through the passage, past the busy lifts, and used the stairs to the ground floor and out. I took off the white coat and sat in the car until twelve-thirty and then returned to the Nursing Home by the side entrance.

The only person in the office was a young girl.

"Dr Camp's asked me to get some papers for him," I said to her. "Get me the files on Mr Chabrier and Mr Petrie, will you?"

"Dr Camp's secretary is at lunch."

"I know she is. But you can find them. Mr Petrie's in room ten."

"All right."

Fraser's file contained everything I'd have expected, from a full medical history to the reports on tests. There were notes in Dr Camp's handwriting and notes written by someone called Dr Wiltshire. I found what I'd been looking for, the report from the laboratory which had shown the Australian antigens. It was the report Dr Camp had shown me. I took it out and put it into my handbag.

As for Mr Chabrier's file, when I'd visited the Nursing Home, a girl had told me that he'd died from rheumatic fever. But the file showed that Mr Chabrier had died of septicaemia.

This piece of information was as important to my mind as the report in my handbag.

The office girl watched me close the Chabrier file. "Didn't you find what you were looking for?"

"What's your name?" I asked her.

"Jenny Bliss."

"How long have you been working here?"

"About a month."

"Haven't you been told that patients' files must not be shown to anyone without permission?"

"I don't remember." Jenny hadn't expected this, and she was looking angry. "I don't know what you mean."

"I mean that files must not be shown to anyone except members of the medical staff or the office staff. I walked in and asked you for two files, and you just let me have them — though you didn't know who I was. If Dr Camp or his secretary found out how careless you've been you'd be in trouble."

Jenny might have turned round and resigned at once, but I didn't think she would. I guessed that it was her first job and that the wages were really good.

"Don't worry," I said. "We all have to learn. You've only just started work, and I'm sure you'll be more careful in future. I'm not going to report you."

"You're not going to tell Miss Davenport?" asked Jenny hopefully.

"No. We'll forget, both of us, that I made this check. All right?"

"Yes. Thanks. . . . Thank you very much."

"You'd better see that I don't meet Miss Davenport as I'm going out."

Jenny rushed to the door and looked out. She waved me on. "It's all right."

I went to Paddington Police Station.

It was one-thirty when I walked in. And luck was still with me. Inspector Barrington was at lunch. The sergeant, Mr Welsh, remembered me because I had sewn up his child's arm after the boy had hurt himself climbing a rough fence.

"There's no need for me to see the Inspector," I said, "if you'd help me, Mr Welsh."

"What can I do for you, Doctor?"

I took the laboratory report from my handbag. "It's a small job for your forensic people. I'd be grateful if they'd examine this paper and let me know what they think of it. I'm more interested in the writing than in anything else."

"I know what you mean, Doctor. The kind of ink, and the kind of pen. What's suspicious about the report, Doctor?"

"I don't know exactly. This kind of thing must have happened to you in your work. Something suspicious about a person — nothing you can describe — just a feeling."

"All right, I'll ask my Inspector to see to it for you."

"How long will it take?"

"Oh, a few days."

"Mr Welsh, I need it today. It concerns a patient, and it's desperately urgent. It'll be delayed if you wait for Inspector Barrington. Couldn't you send the report to your forensic laboratory now, immediately?"

"Well, it's a bit difficult. You see, Doctor, they're . . . we're not really supposed to ask."

"But this is important. I'm sure Inspector Barrington — if he were here — would agree."

"If I knew what it's all about. . . ."

"Just a suspicion, Mr Welsh. The kind of thing you, as a police officer, understand so well."

"I'm not saying that I don't, Doctor. But the Inspector doesn't always see things as I see them."

"Nor as I do; but we're still good friends."

"All right, Doctor, I'll do what I can. Leave it with me."

I let the sergeant have the last word. Had I pressed harder I'd have lost his willingness to help. I needed that forensic job. It would be highly important, whatever they found or didn't find. It would prove whether I'd been right about what happened during the past month or whether I'd let my imagination run away with me. Whichever was right, someone was sure to get hurt. But there'd be less suffering, and for fewer people, if I had not misunderstood the behaviour of the people in whose problems I'd become mixed up.

I wished I could discuss the whole pattern of sickness and fear with my sister — just think aloud and use her insight. But Liz would be playing tennis after school and wouldn't get home before five-thirty. There was nothing I could do for the moment except work.

I went back to my office and saw my patients.

I was about to go home when the telephone rang.

"I hope it is not inconvenient," Madame Taramova's voice came over faintly. "I telephoned because I want to save you trouble, Doctor. Please, I don't need the facelift. I see now that it is foolish. I'm old. It is better for you to arrange the facelift for a young woman. Perhaps you know an actress who needs a new nose."

"Why have you changed your mind, Madame Taramova?"

"It is a pity to waste a doctor on me. Who looks at me? I have no more audiences."

"But the friends who come and stay with you. . . ."

"They're dead, Doctor."

I could not argue with that cool, small voice with its sense of loneliness and old age. Within the past few hours something must have happened to destroy Taramova's dreams of having a circle of famous friends staying in her guest room. Something had made her give up.

I said, "Let's talk it over when I see you. I'll be visiting Elsa."

"Doctor," she said, "I've left Elsa's house. I don't know how to tell you. . . . Elsa's always been very nice. She liked the things I cooked for her. Suddenly she told me, 'Go away, I don't want you here.' I thought she was ill, and that she didn't mean it and I went to the kitchen. Then she came to the kitchen. She was very angry. It was after she had the telephone call. She suddenly became different."

Twelve

When I got home, Inspector Barrington was waiting to see me.

"You've been to see Aureol, Doctor?" asked Barrington.

"Yes."

"You didn't let me know how you got on with her."

"She didn't give me any information, so I had nothing to tell you."

"You're very busy. I quite understand." Barrington managed to make me feel that I was wrong not to have called him. "However, we did something after your visit."

"Waste of time?"

"No, not quite. We sent the right person, a young West

Indian policewoman, to see Aureol," he said to me. "You'll be glad to hear that your story of the attack on Elsa did make her think again."

"She told your girl. . . ."

"She did. But unfortunately she doesn't know much about the man. People call him John. She said he was about one metre eighty-five tall, thin, long dark hair, dark skin, sunglasses. Age uncertain, but could be around forty."

"Did your policewoman find out why Aureol refused to talk until now?"

"It was blackmail, as we thought. Rather curious blackmail. This fellow John appears to know quite a lot about the law. By threatening to have her brother thrown out of the country — which would be terrible for his young family — he gained complete control over Aureol. She'd still be in his power if he didn't sometimes suddenly become unable to control his temper and violent. His final attack on her was in the street, and people saw it. I would expect a similar pattern of pressure in Elsa's case. We must persuade her to help us."

"Inspector, she will talk if you don't push her too fast."

"Why do you say that?"

"I'm in the middle of treating Elsa for an infection which has been giving her high temperatures."

"Are you saying that she isn't fit to be questioned?"

"That is my opinion."

Inspector Barrington kept his eyes on me. "You're sure it's a purely medical opinion?"

"Yes." I hoped he'd believe me. I was not prepared to discuss with him what was, after all, no more than an idea. I was not going to make him suspicious of a person who might or might not be guilty of criminal attacks.

"Very well, we won't call on Elsa this week-end. But I'll telephone you on Monday."

"And it might be a good idea if you kept watch on Elsa's place."

"Oh? Any special reason?"

"A neighbour was staying with her. She's gone."

"I see. Is that all?"

"No. I understand that Elsa had a telephone call which upset her."

"That could be interesting. Oh yes, before I forget." The Inspector put a hand inside a pocket and took out an envelope. "From our forensic laboratory."

I took it eagerly. "Thank you."

"Dr North, I wish you'd tell me about this forensic report. I don't suppose you asked for it just for fun."

"Sorry, it's confidential. It concerns a patient."

"As you borrowed our services, it concerns me too."

"Believe me, there's nothing I can tell you just now — nothing that would interest you."

"But a little later you might perhaps decide to make further use of the police. Is that it? I'd like to hear who this Mr Fraser Petrie is."

I opened the envelope. It contained the laboratory report and a note.

"The line 'Australian Antigen −ve' was written with one pen. The original minus (−) sign was later altered to a plus (+) sign by the addition of a vertical line made with a different pen."

I picked up my bag and hurried out.

I drove straight to one of the most attractive houses on the Regent Canal, hoping that my old chief, Dr Coates, still lived there, and rang the bell. A woman opened it.

"I'm Dr North," I told her. "I'd like to see Dr Coates."

"Is he expecting you?"

"No, but it's urgent."

"Well, I don't know whether the doctor can see you."

"I worked under him at St Mary's Hospital."

"Come in," she said at last.

She left me standing in the hall and went into a room on

the right. I heard laughter and voices. A moment later Dr Coates appeared.

"Norah! what a pleasant surprise. Come and have a drink with us. It's my daughter's birthday."

"It's kind of you, but I can't stay. I need your help. It concerns a seriously sick patient."

He led me into a quiet room at the back of the house.

I gave my famous old chief as complete a history of Fraser's case as I could, without saying too much about my suspicions. When I told him what I'd found in Fraser's medical file, he looked worried. Finally I gave him the laboratory report with its forensic note.

"It sounds serious, I must say. Is there anything in the file on the treatment of the patient?"

"That would be with the nurses. The worrying thing's the laboratory report, isn't it? I'm afraid Fraser is being treated on the basis of that."

"If that is so, the possibilities are quite frightening."

"I haven't said anything to the police."

"I should hope not!" said Coates sharply. "Camp's in trouble because some fool, for reasons we don't know, has changed the minus sign to a plus. Camp should have noticed that there's something strange; but even the best of us can make a mistake, and some of us wouldn't be very happy about admitting it."

"Dr Coates, I'm sure that Fraser will die unless he's removed from the Nursing Home as fast as possible. If he has any chance at all, it'll be in a hospital. Will you take him into St Mary's?"

"I want to help, Norah. But I don't see how I can. I mean, it's an impossible position, isn't it? I can't go and steal patients."

"Fraser has every right to discharge himself from the Nursing Home."

"Of course. But from what you tell me it seems to me that the man's much too ill to walk out."

"He'll have to be helped out."

"By whom?"

"I'd arrange it."

"Doctors don't do that, Norah. You might be going too far."

"Will you take Fraser?"

"Yes. As you say, he has every right to leave the Nursing Home. And it is certainly all right for St Mary's Hospital to admit such an emergency case."

"Thank you, Dr Coates. I'm going to. . . ."

"No," he stopped me. "I don't want to know how the patient is going to get to my hospital. When are we to expect him?"

"Tonight."

Dr Coates returned to his guests, leaving me in the hall with a telephone. My first call was not successful: Mrs Jeff told me that J.J. had just gone out and wouldn't be home until late evening. But she thought he might be at Billy's house.

When I telephoned there, Billy answered. J.J. was not with him.

"What am I going to do?" I thought aloud.

"You sound worried, Doctor. What's the matter?"

"I was hoping he'd be able to help me."

"Well, Doctor, Ted's here. You know — one of the boys. Perhaps he could take a message to J.J. Do you want to talk to him?"

"All right, Billy." Ted; one of the boys who did the gambling in the street. So what?

"Ted O'Malley speaking."

"Mr O'Malley, I'm a friend of J.J.'s."

"His doctor. I know all about you. J.J. said you might come along to gamble and that I was to treat you properly."

"I remember; he said you're as honest as the day is long."

"He's wonderful, J.J. is. What can I do for you then?"

"I need him for a rather special job. It's confidential."

"Sure, I understand."

"Do you know whether any of J.J.'s friends has a van with a back that opens?"

He whistled. "*That* sort of a job!"

"No, Mr O'Malley, you don't understand."

"Oh . . . well. To answer your question, my brother's got a van — a big Leyland."

"Would he lend it to us?"

"For J.J., any time."

"Tonight."

"That's all right. Do you want my brother to pick up the goods for you?"

"Something like that."

"I understand. What time?"

"In an hour and a half?"

"Well that's a bit difficult, Doctor. It'll take me three quarters of an hour to find J.J. Tell me about the job. Maybe my brother could do it without J.J. How many people do you need with the van?"

"Two men."

"Well, I could help."

"All right."

I told Ted as much as he needed to know — enough to make him understand that it was an emergency. I explained what was wanted and when.

"I understand," he said. "Don't worry, Doctor. Eric and I will make a good job of it, just as J.J. would if he was here. I expect Billy would like to know what's happening. Can I tell him?"

"Yes, but he mustn't tell anyone else except J.J."

"All right."

"I'll pay you when I see you."

"Pay us? My brother and I don't take money from our friends and from Billy's friends. We get it in other ways. It's not difficult."

Ever since midday I had been tricking people. I'd lied to the young girl in the office at the Nursing Home, and I'd been less than truthful with Sergeant Welsh and Inspector Barrington.

I telephoned Joanna, and arranged to meet her in the car park of the Nursing Home.

When she arrived, she said, "What's happening, Norah? Is Fraser . . .?" She was so anxious that she could hardly speak.

"Unless we get Fraser out of the Nursing Home and into a hospital he'll die."

"No! We must get Daddy."

"We must keep your father *out* of it. It's essential. Joanna, you're the one who can help Fraser. There's been a mistake, and Fraser's been given the wrong medicines. In law you'd call it a case of criminal negligence."

"It couldn't be — not with Daddy. . . ."

"Listen! If you want your brother to stay alive, don't argue, for God's sake! I'm expecting men with a van who'll take Fraser to hospital, with your help. They're ready for Fraser at St Mary's. The sooner he's there the better his chances of living. Will you do as I ask?"

"Yes, Norah."

"Very well. Go in and ask for Dr Mosin. Say you're Dr Camp's daughter. Tell him that your father's waiting to see him. Bring him out to me."

"What will happen if my father's there?"

"He won't be. Your father's at a meeting."

"How do you know?"

"Never mind, Joanna. You won't meet him; his car isn't here, is it? Now, get Dr Mosin."

"Is that all you want me to do?"

"No. This is just Act One. Be quick. Fraser's got to be out by nine-thirty."

Thirteen

The Pakistani doctor was surprised at finding himself with a stranger instead of Dr Camp, but he accepted my story that I was Fraser's doctor. He didn't ask why I'd wanted him to meet me outside; or perhaps I hadn't given him time to wonder.

"Dr Camp himself is in charge of Mr Petrie's case," he answered my question.

"But you have something to do with it."

"I joined the staff only last week, Dr North."

"You've seen Mr Petrie?"

"Well . . . yes."

"What's your opinion of him?"

"It's difficult to say. I'm not in charge of the case — but I think Mr Petrie's dying."

"Dr Mosin, Mr Petrie is about to leave the Nursing Home. He's discharging himself."

"Impossible! He's too weak to get out of bed."

"Then let's say the patient suddenly decided to go. He arranged a van for himself and telephoned his sister, Mrs Rushton." I turned to Joanna, in the back seat. "His sister arrived. Mr Petrie informed her that he was about to go into a convalescent home."

"You've arranged for him to be admitted . . .?"

"To a teaching hospital. But for your own sake and ours it would be wise if you didn't mention this — or my part in it — to Dr Camp. It must seem that Mr Petrie arranged all this."

"I — I don't understand." Dr Mosin was surprised and worried. "I don't want to have anything to do with this. It's mad!" His hand was on the door. "I think I'll call Dr Camp."

"What can you tell him? That his daughter is here and that she's determined to take her brother away?"

"I don't know. Perhaps if you explained. . . ."

"It'll be better for you if I don't give you all the facts. If you don't know them, Dr Camp won't be able to hold you responsible for letting Mr Petrie go. As you know, you cannot stop a patient who's decided to leave the Nursing Home. In Mr Petrie's case, he's so weak that you *could* stop him by giving him an injection to 'calm him down', for his own good. But as we need your willing help, I'll give you some of the facts." I told Mosin enough to prove to him that Fraser had been receiving the wrong treatment.

He was puzzled, as any good doctor would have been. But he believed, as I'd hoped, that I didn't wish to let everyone know about Dr Camp's medical mistake and that I was dealing with Fraser's situation in this secret way so as to protect Camp from the results of his negligence.

"You're putting me in a very difficult position," Dr Mosin said at last.

"Not if you agree to help . . . Dr Camp's daughter. As far as Dr Camp's concerned, your best protection is to forget that you've met me and everything that's been said."

"This is my first nursing home appointment," begged Mosin. "As a Pakistani I wouldn't have got it if an English doctor had applied. I know Dr Camp well now; unlike many doctors in England, he hates coloured people. Under the new rules, it's going to be even harder for Indians and Pakistanis to become doctors here. They'll have to take tests first. I went to Delhi University, whose medical school is recognised as having top standards. But if Dr Camp accused me of being no good I would never get another job like this."

"Dr Mosin, it's *because* I sympathise with your position that I've asked Dr Camp's daughter to take the responsibility. Dr Camp just won't be able to blame you for letting the patient go, because you clearly couldn't fight his own daughter."

"Yes, I see that."

I gave Mosin time to think.

He knew very well that his whole future might depend on what he decided to do, and he didn't like it. Neither did I.

I said, "I have worked with doctors from India and Pakistan — excellent ones. They're still my friends. I know the disadvantages they have. You don't know me, but I think you now realise that Mr Petrie's life may depend on your decision . . . and I am begging for your help."

At last he said, "I have no choice, Dr North. Have I?"

While Joanna waited for "the boys" with the van I went upstairs. Dr Mosin had sent the nurses to other rooms, and no one saw me enter Fraser's.

He looked at me. I thought he'd recognised me, but he was too weak to show anything. He was worse than I'd feared. And I'd been so sure that I was doing the right thing. Not any more. I'd be lucky if he was still alive after the short trip to the hospital — even with me at his side, ready for an emergency.

"Fraser, please listen. Joanna's here. We're taking you to a teaching hospital. There's nothing for you to worry about; everything's been taken care of."

He slowly moved his head from side to side.

"You'll soon be better," I lied.

"Don't," whispered Fraser, "Don't be . . . silly."

"So you think you're dying? Well, you aren't."

The expression in Fraser's eyes changed. "Here. . . ." I had to bend close to hear what he was trying to say. "Norah . . . no more lies . . . I'm finished. I don't mind . . . I'm used to the idea . . . I'm not afraid. But no more . . . lies."

"Fraser, I swear to God I'm not lying to you now. You're right, you could be finished any moment. But you have a chance, if you fight."

"What with?"

"Fight with your mind. First of all, fight against going to

sleep. You can do it. The reason you're in this trouble is that you've been given the wrong treatment."

There was no need to ask whether he'd understood that one. His eyes opened wide and there was healthy anger in them. Perhaps there was enough anger to keep him alive until we reached the hospital.

I said, "In a few minutes Joanna will come in, and two men. They'll put you in a van. Joanna and I are going to the hospital with you. All right?"

"You win."

No one saw me walk out, and I met no one on the stairs. Dr Mosin had done well. In the car park there was a Leyland van. Ted and his brother, Dr Mosin and Joanna were waiting.

"He's ready," I told them.

"All right," Ted said.

Dr Mosin gave me a file. "The patient's notes."

He'd certainly accepted the situation and was acting as if he were dealing with an ordinary move from one hospital to

another — when the reports and notes on the patient would be sent along with him. Dr Camp would accept that Fraser and Joanna, who had been brought up in a doctor's house, knew this and had asked Dr Mosin to pass the file on.

"Stay here, Dr North," said Mosin. "I'll take them up." He'd understood that it was in his interest that I should not be seen.

"Hullo, Doctor." J.J. put me down on a box behind the driver's seat. "I got here all right. I thought I'd better come to see things go right. . . . This is Charlie, a friend of mine."

"Hullo." I was trembling like a runner before a race. "Your friends have been good."

"Of course. Anyone could guess that Billy's doctor would be doing something quite lawful. I'm not asking any questions, Doctor, but am I right? I mean, when you're not used to doing things like this — if you know what I mean — you can make bad mistakes."

I suddenly realised how right J.J. was; I wasn't safe; not yet. It was essential that I should travel with Fraser and I'd promised him that Joanna would be with us. "J.J., can Charlie drive?" I asked.

"Can he drive! He can drive anything."

"Joanna and I must be in the van with the patient."

"I knew it! We've got to get rid of your car, Doctor."

"Two cars — mine and Joanna's."

"All right, where do you want them?"

"At St Mary's."

"No problem. We'll follow behind the van."

Everything had gone well. They'd put Fraser in the van. He had stayed awake. Dr Coates himself had been waiting for him at the hospital, ready to stay all night. I'd given him Fraser's file.

Then Joanna. I'd been with her when she telephoned Joan. Dr Camp hadn't yet returned home. "Mother, Fraser's much better. He telephoned me . . . said he was leaving the Nursing Home. . . . Daddy's been too anxious. . . . When? . . . Fraser's gone. Well, I went to the Nursing Home and picked him up. . . . That's right. We had dinner at a restaurant and afterwards he took a taxi to the Convalescent Home. . . . Sorry, I haven't got the address. . . . I know I should. I forgot. . . . I was so excited. . . . He'll telephone you. . . . Of course he will. . . . Why should Daddy mind? Fraser's not a child. Look, you know Fraser; he's always done what he wanted. He'll explain to Daddy. . . . Yes, yes, Mum. Jeremy's waiting for me. . . . Sleep well."

And Dr Mosin? Camp could not blame him for anything without people suspecting that he'd been keeping Fraser in the Nursing Home against his will. Camp was going to appear satisfied with Dr Mosin's handling of the situation. He had no choice. Camp just wouldn't be able to complain that Dr Mosin had acted less than correctly.

What would happen next? Camp would learn the news of Fraser's move from Joan. He'd have to take it quietly. And he wouldn't attack Joanna. If he loved anyone at all, it was Joanna, and he'd do nothing that might upset their relationship.

Was everyone safe? Yes, everyone except me. If Fraser died, all of them would put the blame on me, even Joanna.

Early the next morning I would have to telephone Dr Coates. Then Elsa's Dr Singh Awar. I would have to hope that Fraser was still alive, and that Inspector Barrington had arranged for someone to watch Elsa's house.

The telephone rang early the next morning.

"Norah?"

"Good morning, Dr Coates."

"Hope I didn't wake you up."

"No."

"I thought you'd like to know that our patient's alive."

"Thank God for that! Or rather, thank *you*."

"I think he's going to be all right. He should be able to telephone his mother quite soon. But there's one thing. I didn't find anything in his notes from his family doctor."

"He didn't have one."

"That's not usual, is it? Camp looking after his own son?"

"Stepson."

"Yes, I forgot. Different names. If you hadn't interfered, the death certificate wouldn't have shown any family connection. But that's just my nasty mind; I don't believe that Camp meant to kill the young man. A mistake in the laboratory and his own silly mistake. After that, something he wouldn't have admitted even to himself. He should be grateful to you for saving him. Not all of us have such luck."

I telephoned Elsa and felt relieved when she answered.

"How are you?"

"Better, Doctor. Thanks."

"Good. I'll see you later."

"No, don't trouble yourself," she said urgently. "Honestly. My temperature's normal. I'm just going to have breakfast. Really, Doctor, there's no need for you to come."

"Well, take care."

"Oh, I will. I want to go back to work."

"Don't go out just yet."

"I won't."

My next call was to Singh at St George's Hospital.

"How's Elsa?" he asked.

"Elsa's better. I think it's time you and I met at her house."

"I'm very glad. Can we see her today?"

"Yes — eleven?"

"I'm on duty until midday, but. . . ."

"Make it one o'clock, Singh."

"All right, Norah — does she want to see me?"

"I thought it would be best if we . . . just arrived."

"Thank you. I'll be waiting for you outside."

Then I telephoned Derek Harley, who had been at school with Fraser and knew a lot of useful people. His first question was, did I know how Fraser was. Better, I told him.

"It's a funny thing," said Derek. "He was in a great hurry about making his will . . . as if he was dying."

"He made a will?"

"Didn't he tell you? He got the solicitor you recommended."

"What happened?"

"Oh, he wanted us to stop everything to witness his will. Of course we did. I sent one of my clerks; he looked ill. I'm glad he's better."

"Derek, do you know anyone at the Home Office? I just want some advice."

"Let me see. Yes. There's Talbot-Jameson."

"Do you think you could get hold of him? I want to check the position of a doctor from Uganda. He came to London when General Amin threw out the Asians. He's been working in our hospitals ever since."

"What exactly do you want to know, Norah?"

"Whether there's any danger — any danger at all — of his being deported."

When I went to see Billy, he was watching the crowded street below. It was Saturday, and J.J.'s boys were busy with the gambling.

"Percy's still there," said Billy. "You can see he's a policeman from a very long way away."

J.J. had pointed him out to us — a tall young man in an old-fashioned suit, with short curly hair. "Don't worry about Percy," J.J. had told Ted, Eric, Charlie and me. Though Percy was a policeman, he was all right when he was off duty. Percy had grown up around Praed Street as the boys had done. Perhaps. I wasn't so confident about Percy. But I had to trust J.J. I certainly couldn't have found any faults in his plan.

"You all know the man we're after. American Boots, Billy calls him. And we should congratulate Billy here on making a first-class job of noticing him and keeping watch on him." Billy looked happy.

"Our doctor here has done very well, too. She's worked hard to put together all the pieces of the puzzle . . . a very nasty one, if you ask me. There's no one here who can stand people that attack young girls. The doctor says American Boots is mad. Well, we don't care what he is, but we're not going to have him in this part of London. Boys, we're going to get him. We're going to get him tonight." J.J. then gave us a detailed outline of the whole operation.

It might easily succeed — with Elsa's help. Singh's presence and my promises, based on what Mr Talbot-Jameson of the Home Office had told me — that Singh could not be deported from this country — had persuaded Elsa to talk.

Aureol, worried by the attack on Elsa, had told Barrington's policewoman how "John" had blackmailed her. Barrington himself had made it possible for me to guess that the man who had attacked Elsa, if indeed he was the same one, had used the same ways of frightening her. He'd threatened to have Aureol's brother deported. Who was the person Elsa cared about most? Singh, of course — Singh, who had lost his home in Amin's Uganda, and who had no refuge other than Britain. John, of course, had told Elsa that he could have Singh deported.

John had made Elsa leave Singh. It had begun quite simply. They'd met at my surgery. John had come in with a cut hand. After talking to Elsa, he'd changed his mind about getting treatment from one of the doctors and asked Elsa to put a bandage on.

The next time, they'd met in the small restaurant where Elsa went for lunch. She'd told him of her engagement to Singh and talked about the difficulties of finding a flat which they could afford. John had said he might be able to help; a friend of his had some flats.

That's how Elsa had found her cheap home. After she'd moved in, she discovered that John himself owned the house. She was trapped. If John had not had sudden outbursts of violence, his crimes might easily never have been discovered.

Elsa had been feeling miserable about Madame Taramova, who'd been so kind and helpful. She'd never have sent the old lady away if John hadn't telephoned, ordering her to get rid of visitors and wait for him. Elsa hadn't been able to tell Singh and me when John would appear, but she was expecting him at some time during that week-end.

And so we'd prepared for a long wait. Singh was staying with Elsa and I had arranged for Billy's friends to meet me at his house. J.J. had organised a watch on George Cottages. And I would wait at Billy's.

As I sat there I still had deep doubts about who John was. I couldn't get rid of a feeling of guilt. What would happen if we were hunting the wrong man? Though Elsa's description of the man fitted in with Aureol's and Billy's, and even though I myself had seen the back of a man like it, it was still possible that we were about to make a terrible mistake.

I was happy about one thing: at least I had not asked Inspector Barrington to help us this evening. Percy, the plain-clothes man, was still in the street outside. I hoped that Barrington had not sent him, and that he was really off duty.

It was getting dark in the room. Down below, the street-lights were turning bright. Suddenly Billy dropped his binoculars on his blankets and said, "Doctor, Doctor! He's coming!"

Fourteen

"Be careful, Doctor," the man at the street corner said quietly. "He's gone in."

I walked on into the house, ran up the stairs, then stopped half-way, where I could see Elsa's door and the one beside it, the entrance to the electricity meters. No one was there. I crept forward and put Elsa's key in the lock very quietly. There was no light in the hall. Just one table lamp was on in the living room. The door on the other side was half open. Elsa was in bed and Singh was behind the door.

"He's heard something," whispered Elsa. "He must be listening."

He must have been in the place where the electricity meters were. By now he might be inside the cupboard in the hall. Elsa's radio was on. If he'd heard suspicious noises they might have come from the radio.

I pushed my way in beside Singh, out of sight.

I could hear the sounds of traffic coming through the open window of the living room.

Suddenly there was a smell of cigarette smoke. Then his voice. "Get up, you dirty nigger." A Canadian voice.

"No! Don't. . . . John. . . ."

"Who's been here?"

"No one."

"Who?" He was at the bed, tearing at Elsa's hair.

Singh jumped on to that long back; I tried to seize an arm. John swung round and sent Singh crashing into the mirror. Singh attacked again. I was holding on to his coat.

For a second the dark glasses were turned on me. Then he hit me in the chest and I couldn't breathe. I got up off the floor and realised that Singh was safe. John had got away from him and was getting out.

I ran into the living room, and saw him at the window. I suddenly understood: the roof of the oil tank was just below and from there he could jump down easily.

"Doctor, Doctor!" J.J. was calling up to the window. "Are you all right, Doctor?"

"Have you got him?"

"No. But don't worry, he can't get away. There are three of us."

"I'm coming down. Don't let him go."

"No, we won't."

It had been J.J.'s idea to put men at the front and back of George Cottages. It was I who should have thought of that. I'd seen the small shed, and Taramova's basement area, the entrance to the guest room and the cleverly built room itself. I should have guessed, as soon as I'd seen John, that he might try an escape out of the window on to the flat roof and down into his room. I didn't think that there was an escape way inside his flat, but I couldn't be certain.

I turned Elsa's living room lights on. Singh looked all right, except for a cut on his cheek. We looked at each other, and went back to Elsa.

"He'll come again," she said in a small, hopeless voice. "He never gives up."

"Elsa, it's finished," I said. "We know where he is. I'm going to him now. Singh's staying with you."

"Shouldn't I go with you?" asked Singh.

"It isn't necessary. I've got friends down there. You can take care of Elsa."

Ted was on the stairs. "Are you all right, Doctor?"

"Yes."

We walked fast along George Cottages into the Edgware Road. As we turned the corner at the back of Elsa's house, we passed J.J.'s friends, on guard all the way to Madame Taramova's flat.

"We heard the noise," said Ted. "J.J. was very angry, I

can tell you. He thought you'd been killed, Doctor. . . . He said we should have put men right in the flat."

"There would have been too much noise and movement. He'd have noticed it."

J.J. and Charlie were waiting between Taramova's door and John's.

"Are you all right, Doctor?" J.J. asked. He was very worried.

"Yes, I'm all right."

"That's lucky for him," answered J.J. threateningly. "Now we'll break this door down."

"Let's try the normal way, J.J. I'm going to knock."

"I thought you might say that, Doctor. All right. Paddy and Percy, the policeman, will stay with you. Percy's come to help us. It isn't safe to leave you with a man like that."

"Where's Madame Taramova?" I asked.

"Eric's taken her out to a restaurant. We don't want old ladies here if there's going to be a fight, do we? All right, boys. Get ready. The doctor's going to do it like a lady."

I knocked at Madame Taramova's door. It opened almost at once and a polite voice greeted us. "My dear Norah! What a pleasant surprise. John Usher didn't tell me he'd invited you and your friends."

"Where is John, Dr Camp?"

"He's just gone round the corner."

"Let's stop this silly game, Dr Camp. You're under arrest." My voice sounded like a stranger's.

"That's not a very good joke, Norah."

"Dr Camp, it's no joke. As you know, the law gives me the legal right to make a Citizen's Arrest."

He stood there, tall, well dressed, with tidy grey hair. And he was looking down at me with the kind of smile he'd used when Joanna and I had been children . . . pretending to share in our games.

"All right," he said. "I don't know what this is all about, but I won't spoil your fun. A Citizen's Arrest? What am I accused of, young lady?"

"I know you murdered Miss Theresa Petrie. . . ."

"What a stupid statement! I suppose you can prove it?"

"I doubt whether anyone will ever be able to prove it. That's why I'm charging you with the attempted murder of Fraser Petrie."

Fifteen

None of the doctors I know fail to feel sympathetic when they see the effects of serious disease on their patients, and the sad signs of old age. In the few years during which I'd been working as a doctor I too had felt sympathy and had learned, like other doctors, to deal with the sad side of medicine. Yet nothing I'd seen in the course of my work had prepared me for the shock I felt as I watched Dr Camp's face change in front of my eyes.

A few minutes later Inspector Barrington came in with another policeman. I had Liz to thank for that, Liz — who had overheard me making the arrangements with Singh for our meeting at Elsa's. Of course, Percy, the plain-clothes policeman, had been under Barrington's orders.

The policeman searched the rooms and found a bag. In it were the clothes that John or Mr Usher used to be seen in, a black wig and a pair of American boots.

Dr Camp sat down suddenly. He now looked cruel and dangerous. But he still spoke with the voice of an important, educated man.

He said, "I hope, my dear Norah, that you can prove the stupid accusations you've made. I can't imagine how you arrived at such mad ideas."

"I wish they were mad," I told him, and I meant it. I knew what was going to happen to Camp and I was afraid of the misery Joanna and Joan would suffer. "You've been extremely clever, Dr Camp. But you made one fatal mistake; you brought *me* into the murder at the wedding. It was because you brought me in as a doctor that I began to notice a whole lot of small things."

"It was Liz who called my attention to the expression on Miss Theresa's face. She said that the dead woman looked frightened — and that's a little unusual for someone who'd died so suddenly. But it makes sense when one imagines the old lady being persuaded to go to the bedroom and frightened into letting you give her an injection. Before she died she knew, I think, what you were doing to her."

"And what do you *think* I was doing?"

"Carrying out an almost perfect plan. You told people that Theresa had a bad heart and you persuaded her that she had angina — not unusual in an old person. Finally you persuaded her that the excitement of the wedding was about to give her a heart attack and that she needed an injection of coramine. Only, it wasn't coramine you gave her. You'd prepared a special ampoule of adrenalin, which was sure to kill her. You put a box of coramine ampoules on the table. Then you broke one of them, emptied it, and put it beside the box. You then filled your syringe with the adrenalin and injected Miss Theresa. And when she was dead you called Joan and the manager of the Crown Hotel."

Camp looked at Barrington. "She's mad. It's all in her imagination."

"Not quite," I said. "There's more than that. You see, you didn't remove the second broken ampoule — the one which had contained the adrenalin — quickly enough. Mr Smythe, the manager, saw it and remembers it."

"Did *you* see it, Norah?"

"No. By the time I joined you upstairs you'd put it in your pocket. But there are other things you failed to think of.

Miss Theresa was a strong old lady, and used to go out every day, even when it rained. And the whole of Southdown Village knew it."

"From a medical point of view that means nothing."

"Different doctors have different views about that. Another bit of information that I heard concerned Miss Theresa's will. I learned from Fraser that she left all her property to your wife. For perfectly good reasons. But it was this will that decided you on the murder. Had Miss Theresa left her money to Joanna, you couldn't have touched it. What is owned by your wife is relatively easy to inherit, isn't it?"

"Are you trying to say that I was going to kill my own wife?"

"That is what I am saying. You've been working towards Joan's death for quite a long time. You put Joan under great pressure. You always gave her the kind of presents she hated. Worst of all, you made cigarette burns on some of her most beautiful furniture — almost persuading her that she herself had caused the damage. As a result, she became an extremely heavy smoker. I remember you told me that you were afraid that Joan was going mad. So once again, you were trying to bring me into your plans. You tried to destroy either Joan's mind, or her body (through her smoking), or both. Then, when Fraser got jaundice, you worked out a plan for killing him. His death would have been a terrible blow for Joan. Besides, he might easily have left his money to his mother. In fact, Fraser made a will to make sure that you — via Joan — wouldn't get his property. He suspected you."

"Rubbish. Fraser never liked me, but he certainly didn't object to my treating him medically."

"He didn't at first, for his mother's sake. Joan believed you were a wonderful doctor. Fraser didn't want to ruin his mother's marriage. Later, when his illness became very serious, he was in no condition to defend himself against you."

"Ah, we come to the wonderful cure — Fraser walking out of the Nursing Home. Once again, your imagination, I suppose."

"Fact, Dr Camp. Proofs of attempted murder. With one little vertical line made with your pen you changed a minus sign into a plus — changing an ordinary jaundice into an extremely dangerous Australian jaundice, according to the laboratory report. This gave you reasons for keeping away Joan, Joanna and anyone else who might have visited Fraser. And once again this gave you the opportunity of treating the patient with the wrong medicines, which would have killed him if. . . ."

"If you hadn't been such a clever little doctor? There's rather an important thing you've left out of your story. A young doctor like you might be very interested in money. But why should I be? I'm very successful. For years now I've earned at least £20,000 a year." Dr Camp turned to Inspector Barrington. "That does rather destroy her stupid ideas, wouldn't you say?"

"I *wouldn't* say, sir. I expect Dr North will be able to tell us why you need such huge amounts of money. . . . There's one thing I find particularly fascinating, sir. You really tried to make your wife go mad, didn't you? It's rather sad that it caused the death of young Washington."

"Yes," I said. "I know what the noises were that frightened him so much. The footsteps were quite clever — a tape-recording in the attic above Joan's room, switching on when she moved to a certain part of the bed. The door was much simpler; Dr Camp put a magnet in it. It might have worked or not. When anyone left the door slightly open, as people do, the magnet pulled the door. It was Washington's bad luck that the cat went back to its old home. From Miss Theresa's room he'd certainly have heard those footsteps. That's what must have frightened him."

Camp rose from his chair, "I suppose you people can spend this week-end talking. But I can't afford the time. I'm in the middle of some very interesting research. Inspector, if you've quite finished listening to this silly story, I'll go home."

"Sir, I wouldn't try if I were you." Barrington stood up, looking perfectly able to stop any of us leaving the room. "I'd be interested to hear what Dr North has to say about your attacks on two West Indian girls. Why should a doctor want to blackmail girls into sexual relationships and then hurt them?"

I suddenly remembered how I had gradually discovered all the various small pieces of the puzzle, but how I had not recognised their importance until two or three of them had suddenly fitted together — Liz making me notice the frightened expression on Miss Theresa's face. Fraser referring to his stepfather as "the great Dr Camp". Joanna's Jeremy, mentioning Theresa's will and saying that she'd been fond of Joan and Joanna — which suggested that she liked Dr Camp rather less. Joanna, pleased with the mirrors Camp had fixed in her room at the cottage, saying that her stepfather could make anything he wanted to and claiming that there was nobody like him. Joanna, anxious because he'd broken his habit of spending Saturday nights at home. And Billy, who'd noticed the differences in the way young and older people walk and move. Billy, who'd been the first to bring to my attention the fact that "John" or "American Boots" was perhaps older than he appeared.

When this question of age had come up, I'd been able to bring back my own memories of Dr Camp.

I said, "Dr Camp must be at least sixty years old. He used to talk about his student days before the war. He used to tell Joanna and me of his army days. He made it clear that, in his opinion, Britain made the biggest mistake in history when she went to war against Germany. Dr Camp believes in the Nazi ideas of race — that the German and Anglo-Saxon races are better than all others. He hates the fact that we now have a population of mixed races, and he hates coloured people."

Barrington nodded. "That would explain his treatment of

the West Indian girls. But why did he ever start having anything to do with them?"

"Because he needed them for his research."

"Dr North, what do you know about Dr Camp's research?" said Barrington.

"I can't give you facts. But the first thing, which did not seem to have any connection with this case, happened when I visited Fraser at the Nursing Home soon after Dr Camp took him there. I heard that a Mr Chabrier had just died. One of the nurses told me that he'd died of rheumatic fever. But Elsa fell ill with an infection like flu. Meanwhile, I discovered that Elsa had become frightened of hypodermic syringes. And I'd also seen the very modern expensive laboratory Dr Camp had built at his private house. He'd had it built even though he has at least three other laboratories he can use: at the Nursing Home, at his hospital, and one near his office. Even his wife couldn't understand why he'd spent so much money on his private laboratory.

"I got a culture of Elsa's blood. The result was that she had septicaemia. After that I enquired into Mr Chabrier's death. I discovered that Chabrier had, in fact, died of septicaemia."

"That proves nothing," said Camp.

"Not by itself. But with the other pieces of the puzzle it was important. It suggested a connection between your work at the Nursing Home and your private laboratory. It suggested that you are producing cultures in your laboratory and that you had accidentally mixed something from a patient in the Nursing Home up with your private cultures. Finally, it suggests that you've been experimenting on Elsa. She's told me that you injected her with something that made her feel extremely ill."

"Suggestions . . . suggestions," Camp became angry. "Who's going to listen to your stupid suggestions? I. . . ."

"I'm listening, sir," said Barrington. "It's all very interesting. Dr North, could you make a good guess about the kind of research this gentleman's been doing in his expensive private laboratory?"

"Well . . . nothing more than a guess. Inspector, have you heard of biological engineering?"

"Yes, but I know nothing about it."

"Few people do. It's a new science."

"Can you explain it simply, Dr North?"

"I'll try. Recently scientists have learned to take very small pieces of one kind of life and join them up with pieces from other kinds of life, making entirely new combinations which could be extremely dangerous. They could cause a huge increase in dangerous diseases, and prevent the medicines which we now have to kill them from working."

"It's your opinion that Dr Camp's been doing these dangerous experiments? And that he's been using the West Indian girls for them?"

"Yes, I think so."

"Well now, Dr Camp, we seem to have the answer to the question why you needed so much money. You needed it for your laboratory and to buy homes for your West Indian girls. I think we have all we need. Sir, I must ask you. . . ."

"To let you arrest me? To give up all my great scientific work?" Camp suddenly put his hand into the newspapers on the table and took out a gun. "Keep away!" He was walking backwards to the door. "Norah, you're going out first. You're going to tell the men out there that I'll shoot anyone who tries to stop me. Is that clear? Out, Norah, or somebody will get killed if you don't do what I tell you."

"Policemen!" J.J. groaned when he saw us. "They let him go, after all the work we. . . ."

"For God's sake, J.J., get the boys out of his way. He's got a gun and he'll use it."

"My God!" J.J. put two fingers in his mouth and gave a loud whistle. "Ted, hurry! Tell them to get out of the way."

I turned to Camp, who was just behind me. "You heard."

"All right. Stay where you are. I should shoot you, but

you've already done your worst. If I kill you it would only upset Joanna."

Dr Camp came out and suddenly started to run through the empty street.

I heard the sound of brakes, the burst of breaking glass, with a feeling that I'd heard it all before — exactly like that; and a woman's scream and the shouting and the running feet.

Then I was walking along the Edgware Road. The lights of police cars were flashing. All traffic had stopped. A bus stood across the road, and there was a small crowd around the body lying beside it. The grey hair was shining in the light from a shop window.

"Go home, Dr North," said Barrington. "There are enough witnesses of *this* accident. Go home. It's our job now. You're not needed here."

adrenalin, alcohol, ampoule, angina, antigen, attic, blackmail (v.), binoculars, biological, breakdown, bride, certificate, chain-smoking, chart, cloak, convalescent, coramine, cortisone, cremate, cremation, culture, Daddy, dear (n.), deport (v.), depressed (adj.), depression, detective, discharge (v.), emergency, engagement, equipment, facelift, file, forensic, gambling, Great-aunt, hypodermic, idiot, income, infect, infection, infectious, inflation, inherit, inquest, insight, inspector, jaundice, loudspeaker, Madame, magnet, make-up, meter, minus, Mum (n.), negative, negligence, nigger, Nursing Home, outburst, paralysed (adj.), penicillin, plain-clothes, plus, positive, psychopath, reception, registration, relationship, research, rheumatic, scar (n.), septicaemia, sergeant, sexual, solicitor, specialist, stable (n.), stepfather, stepson, stethoscope, strain (n.), subconscious, suicide, sunglasses, surgery, syringe, tape-recording, trolley, trust, undertaker, unemployed, wig, X-ray (v.)